LEG OF LAMB

HOW TO CARVE MEATS

Success in carving depends upon:

1. Meat prepared properly by your meatman (sawing or removal of all bones interfering with carving).

2. Meat cooked correctly—neither under- nor over-done.

3. Meat served on a platter large enough to make handling easy.

TO CARVE: Hold the meat steady with a fork placed out of the way of the knife. Slice across the grain with long, even strokes; pile the slices on one side of the platter; cut enough slices for all the plates before serving.

Porterhouse steak—see page 17 for directions.

Rolled rib roast—cut thin slices across the grain, starting from the right side (cut cords as the roast is sliced down to them).

Standing rib roast of beef—see page 81 for directions.

Leg of lamb—place with shank end to right of carver and thick, meaty portion on far side of platter; cut a few slices from thin side; turn roast so it rests on cut surface; slice down to bone following diagram above; cut parallel to bone to release slices.

Crown roast of lamb—cut between and parallel to the ribs from top of roast toward platter; remove each chop to side of platter; serve 2 chops and portion of the center filling or garnish per serving.

Loin of pork—cut backbone (previously loosened by meatman) away from cooked roast in kitchen; place on platter with ribs toward carver; beginning at right, cut slices close to ribs, making one slice with rib bone, then one without; repeat.

Tongue—place with large end to right of carver; slice off cartilage from large end; make thin, even, parallel slices working toward small end of tongue.

Ham—place with shank end to right of carver and thick meaty portion on far side of platter; cut a few slices from thin side; turn roast so it rests on cut surface; cut small wedge from base near shank end; slice down to bone, following diagram at left below; then cut parallel to bone to release slices.

THE
Family Circle
MEAT
COOKBOOK

Photographs:
Front cover— BROILED SIRLOIN STEAK, *page 16*
Title pages— ROAST LEG OF LAMB, *page 69*
ROLLED RIB ROAST, *page 33*
GLAZED BAKED HAM, *page 86*
Back cover— *(top to bottom)*
CURRIED VEAL IN RICE RING, *page 62*
MERRY-GO-AROUND LAMB, *page 73*
ROAST LOIN OF PORK, *page 82* (Roasted Unfilled)
Garnished with Candied Sweet Potatoes
Black and white photographs of meat cuts,
courtesy, National Live Stock and Meat Board

Contents

The Meat in Your Menus

Whether you are serving a sizzling steak, a roast leg of lamb, or corned-beef hash, meat is the focal point around which you build most menus—and justly so. Generally, the word "meat" is used for beef, veal, lamb, mutton, pork, and ham. Fish and poultry are not included. Nutritionally, there is little difference between "meat" and fish and poultry, but we are including only the first group in this book, reserving the other two for another volume.

Meat is the cornerstone of most meals. You choose it first, then decide on the accompaniments — vegetables, salad, and dessert. There is good reason to give meat this important place in your diet. It is prized not only for its food value, but because of its tempting aroma and appearance—both appetite stimulants. The many kinds and cuts of meat available also make an infinite variety of menus possible.

NUTRITIVE VALUE OF MEAT

Meat is valuable chiefly for its *protein,* the food essential you need for the growth and maintenance of your body. This is found chiefly in meats, sea food, cheese, milk, eggs, and legumes. Smaller amounts are present in cereals, vegetables, and fruits. Meat, however, is important in good diets because its pro-tein content is not only very high, but the protein itself is more valuable.

Proteins are made up of many nitrogen compounds called *amino acids.* As many as 21 different amino acids may enter into combination to form a protein. Thus there are many different kinds of protein, each containing a different group of these acids.

Some amino acids can be manufactured in the body. Some (about 10) are so complex that the body cannot make them.

If a protein contains all of these 10, it is *complete* and is adequate for growth and the repair of tissues. If it contains some but not all the necessary amino acids, it is considered *incomplete.* The protein found in meats is *complete,* that found in vegetable foods is generally more or less *incomplete.* The latter are, however, good supplements, wonderful in rounding out the total protein requirement. The value of supplementary cereal protein is stepped up by the addition of meat protein, making combinations of meat and spaghetti, macaroni, beans, or other "stretchers" excellent contributions to your diet.

Meat is composed of protein, fat, mineral matter, and water. It also contains extractives, vitamins, and traces of carbohydrate. It is a good source of

(continued on next page)

iron and phosphorus and contains a small amount of copper. It is one of the richest sources of the B-vitamins—especially of thiamine, riboflavin, and niacin — and contains some vitamin A. Liver is the richest known source of vitamin A.

The fat of meat supplies energy, vitamins, and fatty acids needed by the body. The number of calories supplied by a serving of meat depends upon the amount of fat. If all the visible fat is eaten, meats add much to the energy content of the diet. With the visible fat removed, meat will fit into a low-calorie diet.

BUYING MEAT

Your success in cooking meat depends first upon your buying knowledge. A large part of your food dollar—as much as 35 to 40%—goes for meats. If you know meat cuts, quality, grades, availability, quantities to buy, the proper way to store meats, and cooking techniques, you will get the best value for your meat money.

Meat Cuts You can recognize meat cuts by their shape, the structure of the muscles, and the shape and size of the bones they contain. Knowing from what section of the animal a particular cut comes helps you to decide on your purchase. The more tender cuts (and the more expensive) come from the supporting muscles that lie along the back bone (chine). The less tender cuts (and less expensive) come from the working muscles such as the neck and shank. The food value of the different kinds and cuts of meat is essentially the same —the cooking methods to be used differ.

Look at the charts on pages 14, 51, 64, and 76. These show you where the various cuts of beef, veal, lamb, and pork come from. The photographs of the actual cuts reproduced throughout the book will show you exactly what to look for when you are buying a particular cut.

Meat Quality and Grading Your guarantee of the wholesomeness of the meat you buy is the *Federal inspection stamp* you see on the meat. All meat shipped in interstate or in foreign commerce must be inspected by trained Government inspectors before and after slaughter. When passed as wholesome, all wholesale carcass cuts are marked with a round purple stamp. The vegetable dye used for stamping is harmless and need not be cut off before cooking. Most of the meat that is not Federally inspected is processed under state and local board-of-health regulations. Most meat, therefore, has passed inspection before you buy it.

Beef, veal, lamb, and cured meats are not only inspected, but generally are graded, either by a Government grader or by the packer. The points used as a basis in grading are:
1. conformation or form
2. finish
3. quality

Animals with good conformation have short, thick, compact bodies with large muscles and a high proportion of meat to bone. Animals with poor conformation are angular and rangy.

Finish is governed by the amount, color, and distribution of fat. This differs for various meats. Well-finished beef has an even layer of fat on the

Federal Stamp, U.S. Grade Stamp

8

exterior of the carcass and the lean is marbled with fat. Veal has little fat either on the exterior of the carcass or distributed through the lean. Its fat is chiefly around the organs such as heart and kidneys. The finish of top quality lamb is similar to that of beef.

Quality is judged by age of animal, color of lean, fineness of grain, and texture of fat. Beef of good quality has a fine grain, creamy white and firm fat, and a bright red color after the cut surface is exposed to the air for a few minutes. Quality veal has grayish-pink flesh and firm, brittle fat. The bones are red, spongy, and soft. Poor quality veal has pale or dark-colored flesh.

Quality lamb is pinkish-red in color with firm, flaky, brittle, white or pinkish fat. The bones are soft, red, and spongy.

Until recently Government grades had not been established for pork. Individual packers, however, have graded it. The newly established U. S. Government grades are not universally used and grade identification is not stamped on retail cuts. Quality pork has a thick external layer of fat (most of which is removed before meat is displayed) and some marbling. The lean is grayish pink in color, the fat is firm and white but not brittle.

Planning Your Meat Buying Meats are now available in many forms. You can have them cut to order by your meatman, or buy them prepackaged fresh, quick-frozen, or canned from your grocery market. In planning your purchases, check your supplies on hand. If you have frozen meat, use it. Don't hold it more than a month unless the temperature of your freezer is 0°F or lower. Check your canned meats. Keep a supply of the family's favorites on your shelves.

The cuts of meat you buy will be influenced by your family's likes and

Rewrap fresh meats wrapped in market paper or store in containers in your meat keeper or under ice-cube compartment.

dislikes, by the amount of time you have for meal preparation, and by the amount of money you want to spend. The price of meat depends a great deal upon supply and demand as well as upon quality. Shop the advertisements in the paper and the meat display cases before you buy. Try new cuts of meat when they offer good buys.

Cuts vary in different parts of the country. The kinds of retail cuts sold in any one locality are usually similar because of custom and demand. The amount and kind of trimming will also vary. In general, however, you will be able to buy most of the cuts shown in this book and you will find recipes using them. Why not experiment with those you haven't tried before?

Quantity To Buy Your family's appetite will determine the amount of meat you buy. Usually one pound of boneless meat such as ground beef will serve four or five. If the meat has medium amounts of bone, count on one-third to one-half pound for a serving. If the cut has much bone or gristle, you'll need one-half to one pound per serving.

(continued on next page)

HOME CARE OF MEAT

Whether you plan to cook your choice for dinner, store it in the refrigerator for another day, or freeze it for future use, follow these simple rules to hold the meat at its peak quality.

To Store Fresh Meat:

- Keep prepackaged smoked or cured meats and sausages in their original wrappers.
- Keep prepackaged fresh meats in their original wrappers but loosen them to allow circulation of air.
- Rewrap fresh meats wrapped in market paper. Keep wrapping loose.
- Store in the meat keeper or directly under the ice-cube compartment as soon as you get home from your shopping trip. A temperature of 35°F to 40°F is best.
- Plan to cook most meats within three days—chopped meat and variety meats such as liver, fresh tongue, and heart should be used within 24 hours.
- Freeze small cuts of meat (see below) if you plan to keep them longer than 2 or 3 days.

To Store Meat in a Refrigerator Freezer Compartment:

- Keep in its cellophane wrap with cardboard backing (helps to hold cut rigid).
- Freeze immediately—not after it has been stored in the refrigerator for a while.
- Plan to use cuts frozen in the ice-cube compartment within five days—cuts frozen in freezer compartment (0° to 10°F) within four weeks.

To Freeze Meat or To Store Quick-Frozen Meat in a Home Freezer:

- Freeze only the freshest and best quality meat (freezing does not improve quality or flavor of meat). Freeze a variety of meats. Choose the less bony cuts, cut into meal-size portions or individual servings before freezing. Wrap in freezer-type materials. Follow the directions for freezing supplied by the freezer manufacturer. Frozen meats should be held at 0°F or lower.
- Prepare meat for freezing immediately upon bringing it home and freeze at 0°F or below.
- Keep in its cellophane wrap with cardboard backing, if already wrapped.
- Overwrap cellophane covering with a moisture-proof freezer paper to keep meat from drying out during storage period. Plain butcher paper is *not* recommended.
- When more than one cut is stored in a single package (such as rib steaks or chops), place a double thickness of freezer paper between each cut— makes them easy to separate when thawing.

STORAGE TIME FOR FROZEN MEATS IN HOME FREEZER	
Ground meats .	Up to 3 months
Fresh pork . .	Up to 6 months
Canned ham (unopened)* .	Up to 3 months
Lamb, veal . .	Up to 9 months
Beef	Up to 12 months
Cooked meats .	Up to 3 months
*Check directions on can.	

To Cook Meat from the Freezer:

- Use frozen meats in the same order as stored. First in should be first out.
- Cook meat in its hard-frozen state, allowing about 20 minutes more cooking time per pound. Or thaw in *unopened* package either in refrigerator or at room temperature. To hasten thawing, set package in front of an electric fan.
- Figure thawing time from size, shape, kind, cut, and wrapping. A large roast

will thaw in 24 to 72 hours in the refrigerator or in 5 to 12 hours at room temperature.

- Follow same time and temperature directions for cooking thawed meats as for fresh.
- Never refreeze meat once it has been thawed.

MEAT COOKERY

The way you cook your meat depends upon the kind of meat and the cut you buy. Meat cookery methods are divided into dry heat, moist heat, and a combination of the two. *Dry-heat cooking* (roasting, baking, broiling, pan-broiling, and frying) is used for tender cuts of meat. This method brings out flavor but does not change the tenderness (or toughness) of the meat. *Moist-heat cooking* (steaming, stewing, and simmering) is used for the less tender cuts of meat. This method helps to convert the tougher connective tissues into gelatin. Long slow cooking is necessary for best results with moist heat. *Braising* or *pot-roasting* is used for many less tender cuts where the flavor of browned meat is desired. In this method the meat is browned first, then water or other liquid is added. The meat is then simmered to tender it.

High temperatures tend to toughen meats and cause too much shrinkage. Meats roasted at a high temperature may shrink as much as 40 to 60%. The same cuts show only a 15 to 20% shrinkage at low temperature, so simmer your stews and roast your beef at the low temperatures we've recommended.

The new electrical appliances such as portable roaster ovens, infra-red broilers, rotisseries, electric casseroles, and deep-fat fryers can add to the fun of cooking. Most of the recipes in this book can be adapted for use with them if you follow the manufacturer's directions.

HERBS IN MEAT COOKERY

The object of seasoning is to enhance, not overpower, the flavor of meat. Use herbs sparingly. Add more only after you have tasted whatever you are making. Avoid too many herb flavors in one dish or at one meal.

Herbs lose their strength, so use them and replace them frequently (no package of herbs should remain on your shelf longer than one year.) Fresh, dried, and powdered herbs vary in strength. Dried herbs are 4 times stronger in flavor than the same measure of fresh. Powdered herbs are about twice as strong as a like amount of crumbled dried leaves.

Herbs You'll Like with Beef: Basil, bay leaf, caraway, celery, chives, dill, garlic, marjoram, onion, paprika, pepper, parsley, rosemary, savory, thyme.

Herbs You'll Like with Veal: Allspice, basil, celery, chives, garlic, lovage, marjoram, onion, paprika, pepper, parsley.

Herbs You'll Like with Lamb: Basil, celery, chervil, chives, cloves (use sparingly), dill, garlic, marjoram, mint, onion, paprika, pepper, parsley, rosemary, savory, thyme.

Herbs You'll Like with Pork: Basil, bay leaf, caraway, chives, coriander, garlic, ginger, marjoram, mustard, onion, oregano, paprika, pepper, parsley, sage, savory, thyme.

Use a table broiler for cool meat cookery.

How to

TO ROAST: *Originally this term was applied to the method of cooking meats before an open fire. Now it is the same as baking. Place roast, fat side up, in shallow roasting pan (use rack under boneless cuts). Do not add water or cover. Season, if you wish. Roast at 325° F for time needed (use meat thermometer for best results). Do not baste.*

TO BROIL: *Set oven regulator at "broil"; preheat broiler (if your range has no regulator, heat broiler 5 minutes). Score fat edges every 2 inches to prevent curling. Place meat on broiler rack 3 to 4 inches from unit or tip of flame (2-inch steaks should be 6 inches from heat). Broil until top is brown and meat is about half done; turn; broil until meat is as you like it.*

TO PAN-BROIL: *Heat heavy frying pan almost to smoking point. Do not add fat, but sprinkle pan with salt, if you wish. Score fat edges every 2 inches to prevent curling. Place meat in pan; pan-broil until meat is brown; turn (stick fork or tongs into fat rather than meat itself to keep juices in); brown second side. Lower heat; cook on each side until meat is the way you like it.*

TO FRY: *Melt enough fat (this is best method for meats lacking fat, such as round steak and liver) to cover bottom of pan with film of fat; season meat with salt and pepper, if desired; place in pan; fry until meat is brown; turn (use tongs); brown second side; lower heat; cook on each side until meat is as you like it.*

Cook Meats

TO DEEP-FAT FRY: *Pour melted vegetable shortening, lard, or salad oil into kettle to depth sufficient to cover meat to be cooked, or into electric fryer following manufacturer's directions. Prepare meat (usually by coating with mixture of bread or cracker crumbs). Heat fat to temperature of 365°F-375°F; fry meat for time required, drain.*

TO BRAISE: *Rub meat with SEASONED FLOUR; brown (to develop flavor) in a little fat in heavy frying pan with tight-fitting cover or Dutch oven over medium heat. When meat is well browned, add small amount of liquid (water, vegetable juices, stock, or canned soups, if desired); cover tightly; simmer (to make meat tender) until meat is tender when pierced with 2-tine fork.*

TO STEW: *Cover meat with water; cover pan; simmer until meat is tender when pierced with 2-tine fork. For a brown stew, dust meat with SEASONED FLOUR; brown in small amount hot fat before adding liquid. When large pieces of meat are cooked in water, they are described as "boiled." A simmering rather than a boiling temperature, however, is used in meat cookery.*

TO PRESSURE-COOK: *Place meat in pressure cooker; add liquid (usually ½ to 1 cup) and other ingredients; cover cooker; cook at pressure and for length of time required in recipe; cool cooker according to manufacturer's directions; remove cover; make gravy, if needed, without pressure. Use when quick moist-heat cooking is needed.*

Beef

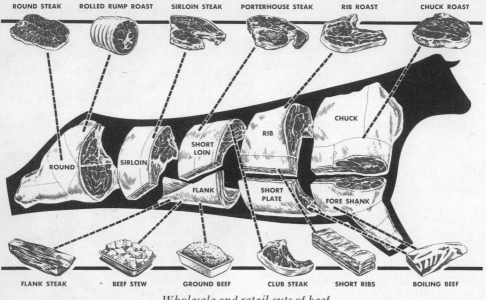

ROUND STEAK · ROLLED RUMP ROAST · SIRLOIN STEAK · PORTERHOUSE STEAK · RIB ROAST · CHUCK ROAST

CHUCK · RIB · SHORT LOIN · SIRLOIN · ROUND · FLANK · SHORT PLATE · FORE SHANK

FLANK STEAK · BEEF STEW · GROUND BEEF · CLUB STEAK · SHORT RIBS · BOILING BEEF

Wholesale and retail cuts of beef

Quality beef comes from cattle bred for meat. Cuts from well-fed yearlings or two-year-olds are usually the best.

Beef that is aged or ripened is juicier and tenderer than freshly slaughtered meat. Aging is brought about by hanging prime or choice grades of beef in cold storage at a temperature of about 36° F for varying lengths of time. Experiments have shown that 15 to 20 days of hanging will produce tender beef. Today, scientific shortcuts such as the *Tenderay* process are used to speed up aging.

Beef usually is graded either by United States Government graders or by the packer. When graded by a Federal grader it is designated as U. S. Prime, U. S. Choice, U. S. Good, U. S. Commercial, and U. S. Utility. The grades U. S. Cutter and U. S. Canner are not found in meat departments. Many packers grade their own beef using various trade names to indicate grade. This is known as "branded beef."

The higher grades of beef have better flavor and are more tender. Certain cuts are more palatable than other cuts from the same animal. When the beef carcass is cut up the tender meat is separated from the tough meat and thick areas are separated from thin because the methods of cooking differ for each. The muscles are cut across the grain to make the meat tenderer.

Wholesale and retail cuts of beef vary, but the variations are small and, generally, do not affect cooking techniques.

Kosher beef is prepared according to the Mosaic law for the Jewish trade. Only the forequarter is used and the meat is usually sold within three days after slaughter.

Beef cuts are often classified as: most tender cuts (rib, loin); medium tender cuts (chuck, round, rump); least tender cuts (flank, brisket, neck, plate, shank). Practically all meats become tender when properly cooked.

Steaks

Thick, juicy steak is as American as apple pie—and it can be as varied as you wish. There are about 15 different cuts of beef that you can cook as steak.

The best quality steak is cherry-red in color and is firm to the touch. The lean is velvety, fine-grained, with little veins of creamy-white fat running through it, and the cut has a collar of just enough flaky fat surrounding it to make it perfect eating. There is little or no waste in a well-trimmed steak.

To Buy For broiling or pan-broiling, buy *sirloin, tenderloin* (filet mignon), *porterhouse, T-bone, club* (Delmonico), or *rib* steaks of U.S. Prime, U.S. Choice, and U.S. Good grades. You can also broil or pan-fry *round, rump, chuck,* or *flank* steak of U.S. Prime or U.S. Choice grades if you like your steaks medium or well done.

For braising, buy *sirloin* of U.S. Commercial and U.S. Utility grades or *round* (all cuts), *chuck* (arm or blade), or *flank* of U.S. Good, U.S. Commercial, or U.S. Utility grades (of course, you can use prime, choice, or good if you like). The type of steak you buy will depend upon the way you plan to cook it and the size of your family. Buy a steak cut 1 to 2 inches thick for broiling or braising or ½ to 1 inch thick for pan-frying. Allow about ¾ pound, bone-in, or about ½ pound, boned, per serving. The weights of steaks vary depending upon the quality of the animal and the way your meatman trims them.

SIRLOIN STEAK (full cut) This is an excellent buy for family eating or out-of-door steak parties, for it has comparatively little bone. The size and shape of the bone varies according to the location from which the steak is cut and the steak is often identified by the type of bone. Beginning at the round end of the sirloin, the first steaks cut are known as wedge-bone, then as round-bone, double-bone, and pin-bone. Bottom sirloin is less tender than top. A 1½-inch-thick full cut weighs 3 to 4½ pounds; a 2-inch-thick full cut, 4 to 5½ pounds. A 2-inch-thick cut will serve 6 generously.

PORTERHOUSE STEAK This familiar cut with a T-shape bone has the largest piece of tenderloin, a large meaty eye portion, and a very small tailpiece. A 1½-inch-thick steak weighs about 3 pounds and will serve 3 generously. It is sometimes sold as a T-bone steak.

T-BONE STEAK This is smaller than a porterhouse but looks much like it and is sometimes sold as a porterhouse steak. A 1½-inch-thick cut weighs 1½ to 2 pounds and will serve 2 to 3.

CLUB STEAK (DELMONICO) This is the smallest steak in the short loin. It is triangular in shape and has little or no tenderloin. A 1½-inch-thick steak weighs 12 ounces to 1 pound and makes 1 to 2 servings.

RIB STEAK (sometimes called club steak) This is sliced from the eye of the rib roast and is usually boneless, but may contain rib bone. The best rib steaks are cut from the loin end. This cut is favored for pan-frying, broiling, or grilling out of doors. A steak cut ¾-inch thick weighs 10 to 12 ounces and makes 1 generous serving.

TENDERLOIN or FILET MIGNON This is a small, boneless and very tender and expensive steak cut from the beef tenderloin that lies just inside the ribs. Tenderloin steaks, when cut 1 inch thick, weigh about 6 ounces. Serve 2 thin or 1 thick steak per person.

Wedge-bone sirloin steak   *Porterhouse steak*   *T-bone steak*

MINUTE STEAK   Generally this is a ½-inch-thick cut from the loin or rib, flattened to ¼-inch thickness. It is available fresh and frozen. Pan-broil. Use 1 steak per serving.

To Store Wrap steaks loosely in waxed paper or aluminum foil. Store flat in your refrigerator. Use within 5 days. Steaks can be kept longer if frozen in freezer or frozen-food compartment of your refrigerator. Thaw in refrigerator or cook while still frozen.

To Cook Steaks cook to perfection in the broiler of your gas or electric range or in a heavy frying pan without fat.

TO BROIL: Turn oven regulator to *broil* and preheat broiler, following manufacturer's directions. If your range has no regulator, heat broiler for 5 minutes. Score fat edges of meat every 2 inches to prevent curling. Place steak on broiler rack; broil, with top of meat about 3 inches from unit or tip of flame, for half the time called for in TIME-TABLE, page 17; season cooked side with salt and pepper. Stick fork in fat portion and turn steak once; finish broiling. Season second side; spread generously with butter or margarine; serve piping hot.

TO PAN-BROIL: Heat heavy frying pan to almost smoking. Do not add fat, but sprinkle pan lightly with salt, if you wish. Brown scored steak in hot pan; turn; brown other side. Lower heat and cook on each side until steak is done the way you like it. Season the same as for oven-broiled steak; serve at once.

TO PAN-FRY: Season steak with salt and pepper; brown on both sides in hot fat in large heavy frying pan over medium heat; reduce heat; continue cooking until meat is cooked the way you like it.

TO BRAISE: Season steak with salt and pepper; brown on both sides in hot fat in large heavy frying pan with tight-fitting cover over medium heat; add a small amount of hot water, tomato juice, consomme, or bouillon; cover tightly; simmer until meat is cooked the way you like it.

TO BROIL LESS TENDER CUTS OF BEEF: Less tender cuts of beef such as round, chuck, or flank steak can be broiled also if they are tenderized first. Many methods are used:

Pounding with a meat mallet or edge of saucer to break up the tissues. Cubing—a commercial method for doing the same thing.

Grinding (see GROUND BEEF, page 18).

Soaking (marinating) in an acid such as tomato juice, vinegar, or wine.

Tenderizing with a meat-tenderizing salt (a commercial product containing a substance, papain, found in the papaya fruit, that softens protein tissues).

To Use Meat-Tenderizing Salt Sprinkle steak lightly and evenly on both sides with the salt; prick the steak clear through in several places with a 2-tine fork (the same as pricking a pic shell). For each ½-inch thickness of steak,

16

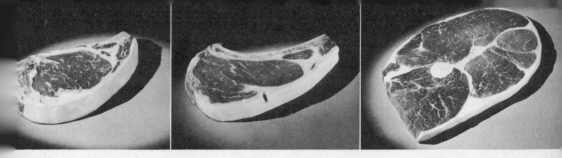

Club steak   Rib steak   Round steak

TIMETABLE*
Broiling Steaks†

(Broil each side for half of total time)

Thickness	Rare	Medium
1 inch	8-10 min.	12-14 min.
1½ inches	14-16 min.	18-20 min.
2 inches	30-35 min.	40-50 min.

(For chuck, blade, or round steak, when using meat tenderizer)‡

1 inch	10-12 min.	12-14 min.
1½ inches	15 min.	20 min.
2 inches	20-25 min.	25-30 min.

Broiling Tenderloin† (Filet Mignon)

1 inch	Rare	8 min.
	Medium	12-16 min.
1½ inches	Rare	12-16 min.
	Medium	16-20 min.

*All times given are approximate, since the terms "rare," "medium," and "well done" are relative. Cook your steaks the way you like them using these figures as guides.

†Time is for chilled meat from the refrigerator.

‡Time is for treated steaks.

allow ½ hour's tenderizing time before broiling. For example, if your steak is 1 inch thick, take it out of the refrigerator 1 hour before you want to broil it. Treat it on both sides with the tenderizing salt, cover with waxed paper, and let stand at room temperature.

Watch your time, for when you start broiling, the heat will immediately kill the papaya's tenderizing action, and you'll want the steak to go into the broiler at its peak of tenderness. If you need to hold the uncooked steak for a while after the salt has been sprinkled on, put it in the refrigerator. The chilling will slow up tenderizing. When ready to cook, broil to juicy tenderness —rare, medium, well done, following the TIMETABLE at left.

To Carve Club and rib steaks need no special carving by the server. The center bone in a porterhouse, T-bone, or sirloin steak should be removed before carving and serving. To remove bone, cut around it with tip of sharp-bladed knife. Remove bone to side of platter. With sharp carving knife, cut about ¾-inch-thick slices straight across steak. Serve each person a cut of outside meat and a cut of tenderloin.

Broiled Flank Steak (London Broil)*

Makes 4 to 5 servings

   1 flank steak (about 1½ pounds)
   Salt
   Pepper
   Softened butter

1. Place steak on broiler rack in heated broiler oven; broil, with top of meat 3 inches from unit or tip of flame, 2 to 3 minutes on each side. (Steak will be rare.)

2. Place on heated platter; season to taste with salt and pepper; brush with softened butter.

3. Slice diagonally across the grain.

*Requires aged, top-quality flank steak.

Ground Beef

Since that day at the Saint Louis Fair in 1904 when the "hamburger" sandwich was introduced, "hamburger" or ground beef has been a mainstay in American meals. Ground beef is a thrifty meat buy, a good mixer with starchy foods or extenders, and the basis for many quick-and-easy-to-prepare meals.

To Buy *Sirloin tip, round, chuck, neck, shank, short plate, brisket,* or trimmings from other cuts may be ground and sold as *ground beef* or "hamburger." The quality of ground beef depends upon the cut of meat, the grade of meat, and the amount of fat. Freshly ground beef is bright red in color. Ground ready-to-use beef comes in 2 styles—regular (contains up to 25% fat) and lean (contains no more than 12% fat). Both types are ground twice.

The quality of meat ground-to-order, of course, depends upon your choice of cut. Round steak makes lean ground beef, chuck the juiciest. If the meat is very lean, have 2 ounces of suet ground with each pound of meat. The number of grindings depends upon the use you make of the meat. For very juicy, light, and tender patties, use meat ground only once; for meat loaves and meat balls have the meat ground 2 or 3 times, using the fine setting on the grinder. Meat patties weighing 2 or 3 ounces each are also sold quick-frozen in packages.

Buy 1 pound of ground beef for 4 or 5 servings. If you use extenders, 1 pound will make 4 to 8 servings.

To Store Wrap loosely in waxed paper; store in coldest part of your refrigerator; use within 24 hours. If you plan to store ground beef for a longer time, shape into patties; stack between squares of freezer paper; wrap in aluminum foil or freezer paper; store in your freezer (use within 3 months) or in the freezing compartment of your refrigerator (use within a week).

TIMETABLE*
Broiling Meat Patties†

(Broil each side for half of total time)

Thickness			
½ inch	Rare	4- 6 minutes	
	Medium	8-10 minutes	
1 inch	Rare	8-10 minutes	
	Medium	14-16 minutes	

Pan-Broiling and Pan-Frying
Meat Patties†

½ inch	Rare	2 minutes
	Medium	6 minutes
1 inch	Rare	4 minutes
	Medium	8 minutes

All times given are approximate, since the terms "rare," "medium," and "well done" are relative. Cook your meat patties the way you like them using these figures as guides.

†Time is for chilled meat from the refrigerator.*

Family Circle's Patties

Makes 4 servings

1 pound ground beef
1 small onion, finely chopped (¼ cup)
½ teaspoon salt
¼ teaspoon celery salt
¼ teaspoon pepper

1. Combine all ingredients in medium-size bowl; toss together lightly with 2-tine fork. (Do not overmix.)
2. Shape into 4 thick patties about 3x1, or into 8 thin patties about 3x½.
TO PAN-FRY: Melt enough fat (about 2 tablespoons) just to cover bottom of medium-size frying pan. Fry over medium heat on both sides until meat is cooked the way you like it. For cooking time, see TIMETABLE at left.

(continued on page 20)

Right—LASAGNE, page 22

TO PAN-BROIL: Heat frying pan or griddle until sizzling hot; rub lightly with fat, or sprinkle with salt, if desired; brown patties on both sides over medium heat. For cooking time, see TIMETABLE, page 18.

TO BROIL: Arrange thick patties on heated broiler rack. Broil, with top of meat 3 inches from unit or tip of flame, turning once. For cooking time, see TIMETABLE, page 18.

VARIATIONS

Extra-Juicy Patties Add 3 tablespoons cream or undiluted evaporated milk in Step 1.

Gourmet Patties Cook FAMILY CIRCLE'S PATTIES your favorite way; serve on heated platter; spread with any of the BUTTERS on page 130.

Cheese-Filled Patties Make 8 thin patties; spread 4 patties with blue-cheese spread; top each with a remaining patty; cook the way you like them.

Relish Surprises Make 8 thin patties; spread 4 patties with India relish; top each with a remaining patty; cook the way you like them.

Barbecued Patties Brown patties on both sides in large heavy frying pan over medium heat; spoon HOT BARBECUE SAUCE, page 131, over meat; cover tightly; simmer 20 minutes.

CITY-BURGERS

Herb Patties Add ¼ teaspoon sage; ¼ teaspoon marjoram; 1 egg, unbeaten; and ¼ cup soft bread crumbs in Step 1.

SAUCES TO SERVE WITH MEAT PATTIES

FLORENTINE SAUCE, page 129; BERNAISE SAUCE, page 130; TOMATO SAUCE, page 130; MADEIRA-MUSHROOM SAUCE, page 129.

Quick 'n' Easy Patties

Shape meat into patties just as it comes from your grocery market; sprinkle each patty with salt, pepper, and garlic salt; broil, pan-broil, or fry; cook them the way you like them.

Country-Burgers

Makes 4 servings

1 pound ground beef
1 teaspoon dry mustard
½ teaspoon salt
⅛ teaspoon pepper
2 tablespoons finely chopped green pepper
½ cup milk
1 tablespoon butter or margarine
1 can condensed cream of mushroom soup

1. Combine beef, mustard, salt, pepper, green pepper, and milk in medium-size bowl; toss together lightly with 2-tine fork. (Do not overmix.)
2. Shape into 4 patties.
3. Melt butter or margarine in large frying pan with tight-fitting cover; brown patties over medium heat on both sides.
4. Pour soup into pan; cover tightly.
5. Bring to boiling; reduce heat; simmer, basting patties occasionally with soup, 10 to 15 minutes, or until meat is cooked the way you like it.

Hamburger Grill

Makes 4 servings

½ pound ground beef
1 small onion, finely chopped (¼ cup)
Few drops Worcestershire sauce
½ teaspoon salt
⅛ teaspoon pepper
12 pineapple chunks (from 14-ounce can)
8 chicken livers
8 small mushroom caps
8 slices bacon

1. Combine beef, onion, Worcestershire sauce, salt, and pepper in medium-size bowl; toss together lightly with 2-tine fork. (Do not overmix.)
2. Shape into 8 small balls.
3. String on 7-inch metal skewer a pineapple chunk, meatball, chicken liver, and mushroom cap; repeat; end with pineapple; wrap food on skewer with 2 bacon strips.
4. Repeat to fill 4 skewers.
5. Broil, with top of meat 4 inches from unit or tip of flame, 4 to 5 minutes on each side, or until meat balls and chicken livers are cooked the way you like them.

City-Burgers

Makes 4 servings

1 pound ground beef
1 medium-size onion, finely chopped (½ cup)
1 teaspoon salt
½ teaspoon marjoram
⅛ teaspoon pepper
8 slices buttered toast
¼ cup (½ stick) butter or margarine
1 tablespoon bottled thick meat sauce
8 radish slices
8 small pickled onions

1. Combine beef, onion, salt, marjoram, and pepper in medium-size bowl;

toss together lightly with 2-tine fork. (Do not overmix.)
2. Spread mixture evenly on toast slices, bringing it to edges.
3. Broil, with top of meat about 4 inches from unit or tip of flame, 3 to 5 minutes, or until meat is cooked the way you like it.
4. Melt butter or margarine in small saucepan while meat broils; stir in meat sauce; spoon hot mixture over meat.
5. Stack 2 burgers on each plate; garnish with kabobs of radish slices and pickled onions.

Savory Meat Sauce

Makes about 10 cups sauce

1 large onion, chopped (1 cup)
2 cloves of garlic, minced
¼ cup salad or olive oil
2 pounds ground beef
8 cups (4 cans, about 1 pound each) tomatoes
2 cans (6 ounces each) tomato paste
½ cup water
½ cup chopped celery
¼ cup chopped parsley
1½ tablespoons salt
2 teaspoons sugar
1 teaspoon basil
¼ teaspoon pepper
2 bay leaves

1. Saute onion and garlic in hot oil in large kettle over low heat 5 minutes; add beef; brown over medium heat, breaking up meat with fork as it cooks.
2. Stir in remaining ingredients.
3. Bring mixture to boiling; reduce heat; simmer, stirring occasionally, 3 hours, or until sauce is thick.
4. Remove bay leaves; skim; or chill, then skim off hardened fat.
5. Store, covered, in refrigerator, or freeze in freezer containers. Use with spaghetti, noodles, rice, or macaroni.

Lasagne

Bake at 350° F about 30 minutes . . .
Makes 8 large servings

- 1 pound lasagne noodles (1½-inch-wide noodles)
- 1 tablespoon salad oil
- 5 cups **Savory Meat Sauce,** page 21
- 2 cups (1 pound) ricotta cheese
  Or: 2 cups (1 pound) cream-style cottage cheese
- 2 packages (8 ounces each) Mozzarella cheese, thinly sliced
- ½ cup grated Parmesan cheese

1. Slide lasagne-noodle strips, without breaking, into large kettle half filled with boiling salted water to which salad oil has been added (helps keep noodles from sticking).
2. Cook, stirring often with a wooden spoon, 15 minutes, or until almost tender; drain; cover with cold water.
3. Line bottom of lightly oiled baking dish, 13x9x2, with single layer drained lasagne noodles (lift each noodle from water separately); spoon over about ¼ of the meat sauce and ricotta or cottage cheese; top with ¼ of the Mozzarella and Parmesan cheeses; repeat to make 4 layers, ending with cheese topping.

JOHNNYCAKE CASSEROLE

4. Bake in moderate oven (350°F) 30 minutes, or until hot. See photograph, page 19.

Johnnycake Casserole

Bake at 450°F for 20 to 25 minutes...
Makes 4 to 6 servings

Meat Mixture
- 2 tablespoons butter or margarine
- 1 large onion, chopped (1 cup)
- 1 pound ground beef
- 2 tablespoons flour
- 1 teaspoon salt
- ⅛ teaspoon pepper
- 1 can (about 1 pound) peas
- 1 can condensed cream of celery soup

Johnnycake Topping
- ¾ cup corn meal
- 1 tablespoon flour
- 1 tablespoon sugar
- 1½ teaspoons baking powder
- ½ teaspoon salt
- ⅓ cup milk
- 1 egg, slightly beaten
- 1 tablespoon salad oil

1. MAKE MEAT MIXTURE: Melt butter or margarine in large heavy frying pan; saute onion over low heat 10 to 15 minutes, or just until tender; add beef; brown over medium heat, breaking up meat with 2-tine fork as it cooks.
2. Blend in flour, salt, and pepper; stir in undrained peas and soup.
3. Cook over low heat, stirring constantly, until mixture thickens and boils 1 minute; keep hot.
4. MAKE JOHNNYCAKE TOPPING: Measure corn meal, flour, sugar, baking powder, and salt into sifter; sift into medium-size bowl.
5. Stir in milk, egg, and salad oil.
6. Pour hot meat mixture into 2½-quart baking dish; spoon johnnycake batter evenly over top.
7. Bake in hot oven (450°F) 20 to 25 minutes, or until topping is brown.

Party Hamburgers

Bake at 450°F for 20 to 25 minutes...
Makes 4 servings

1 pound ground beef
1 small onion, finely chopped (¼ cup)
1 teaspoon salt
⅛ teaspoon pepper
½ cup chili sauce
4 slices bacon
4 canned apricot halves, drained

1. Combine beef, onion, salt, pepper, and chili sauce in medium-size bowl; toss together lightly with 2-tine fork. (Do not overmix.)
2. Shape into 4 patties; wrap each with strip of bacon; fasten with wooden pick or small skewer; top each with apricot half; place in shallow baking pan.
3. Bake in hot oven (450°F) 20 to 25 minutes, or until meat is cooked the way you like it.

Italian Cheeseburgers

Makes 4 servings

8 thick slices Italian bread
Butter or margarine
Garlic salt
1 pound ground beef
¼ cup catsup
1 teaspoon salt
½ teaspoon basil
¼ teaspoon oregano or thyme
⅛ teaspoon pepper
1 small onion, finely chopped (¼ cup)
8 slices Mozzarella cheese

1. Toast bread slices on one side in broiler; spread untoasted sides with butter or margarine; sprinkle lightly with garlic salt; save for Step 5.
2. Combine beef, catsup, salt, basil, oregano or thyme, pepper, and onion in medium-size bowl; toss together lightly with 2-tine fork. (Do not overmix.)

3. Shape into 8 oval patties the same size as toast slices.
4. Broil, with top of meat about 4 inches from unit or tip of flame, 3 to 5 minutes on each side, or until meat is cooked the way you like it.
5. Place broiled hamburgers on untoasted sides of bread slices; top with cheese slices; broil 2 to 3 minutes longer, or just until cheese melts.

Scotch Casserole with Biscuits

Bake at 450°F for 20 to 25 minutes...
Makes 4 servings

2 tablespoons butter or margarine
1 large onion, finely chopped (1 cup)
1 pound ground beef
2 tablespoons flour
1½ teaspoons salt
⅛ teaspoon pepper
1 tall can evaporated milk
2 cups drained cooked or canned peas
2 pimientos, diced
1 cup biscuit mix
⅓ cup milk

1. Melt butter or margarine in medium-size frying pan; saute onion over low heat 10 to 15 minutes, or just until tender; add beef; brown over medium heat, breaking up meat with 2-tine fork as it cooks.
2. Blend in flour, salt, and pepper; stir in milk and peas.
3. Simmer, stirring constantly, 5 minutes; stir in pimientos; keep mixture hot.
4. Prepare biscuits according to directions on package of mix, using ⅓ cup milk.
5. Spoon hot meat mixture into 2-quart casserole; arrange biscuits on top.
6. Bake in hot oven (450°F) 20 to 25 minutes, or until biscuits are golden-brown.

Western Scramble

Makes 4 servings

1 large onion, chopped (1 cup)
1 clove of garlic, minced
2 tablespoons salad oil or olive oil
½ pound ground beef
2 tablespoons catsup
1 teaspoon salt
⅛ teaspoon pepper
1 cup coarsely chopped spinach
 leaves
4 eggs, well beaten
4 slices buttered rye-bread toast

1.   Saute onion and garlic in hot oil in large heavy frying pan over low heat 10 to 15 minutes, or just until onion is tender.
2.   Add beef, catsup, salt, and pepper; cook, breaking up meat with 2-tine fork.
3.   Stir in spinach leaves and eggs; cook, stirring constantly, until eggs are scrambled and spinach is wilted.
4.   Spoon over slices of toasted rye bread; serve with chili sauce, if desired.

Stuffed Cabbage

Bake at 375°F about 1½ hours . . . Makes 8 rolls

1 medium-size head of cabbage
1 can (1 pound, 13 ounces) sauerkraut
2 cups (about 1-pound can) tomatoes
1 large onion, sliced
⅓ cup sugar
½ teaspoon rosemary
¼ teaspoon oregano
1 pound ground beef
½ cup raw rice
1 large onion, finely chopped (1 cup)
1½ teaspoons salt
1 teaspoon celery salt
¼ teaspoon pepper
 Dash of cayenne
2 tablespoons melted bacon drippings
 or fat

1.   Remove core of cabbage head; pull off and discard any imperfect outside leaves; starting at core end, remove 8 large cabbage leaves by gently loosening 1 at a time from head; with paring knife trim heavy stalks or veins until even with leaf. (Use remaining cabbage for another meal.)
2.   Steam cabbage leaves, covered, in small amount of boiling salted water for 8 minutes; remove; drain; save for Step 5.
3.   Combine sauerkraut, tomatoes, sliced onion, sugar, rosemary, and oregano in medium-size bowl; save for Step 6.
4.   Combine meat, rice, chopped onion, salt, celery salt, pepper, cayenne, and drippings or fat in medium-size bowl; toss together lightly with 2-tine fork. (Do not overmix.)
5.   Spoon equal amounts of meat mixture onto center of each cabbage leaf; fold opposite edges over; then fold top and bottom edges; fasten with wooden picks.
6.   Place, folded side down, in baking dish, 13x9x2, alternating rolls with sauerkraut mixture; cover tightly.
7.   Bake in moderate oven (375°F) 1 hour; remove cover; continue baking 30 minutes.

Beef Ring, Bernaise

Bake at 400°F about 40 minutes . . . Makes 6 servings

1½ pounds ground beef
1 large onion, finely chopped (1 cup)
1½ cups (about 3 slices) soft bread crumbs
1½ teaspoons salt
1 teaspoon dry mustard
½ teaspoon pepper
½ teaspoon sage
1 egg, unbeaten
1 cup tomato juice
3 slices bacon
Bernaise Sauce, page 130

1. Combine beef, onion, bread crumbs, salt, mustard, pepper, sage, egg, and tomato juice in medium-size bowl; toss together lightly with 2-tine fork. (Do not overmix.)

2. Spoon meat mixture into oiled 1½-quart ring mold; spread evenly; arrange bacon slices on top.

3. Bake in moderately hot oven (400°F) 40 minutes, or until meat shrinks from sides of mold and is cooked the way you like it.

4. Turn out onto heated platter; serve with BERNAISE SAUCE.

Stuffed Beef Roll

Bake at 350°F about 1 hour...
Makes 8 servings

  2 pounds ground beef
  1 medium-size onion, chopped (½ cup)
  ½ cup catsup
  1 egg, unbeaten
  1 teaspoon salt
  ⅛ teaspoon pepper
  Bread and Butter Stuffing, page 140

1. Combine beef, onion, catsup, egg, salt, and pepper in medium-size bowl; toss together lightly with 2-tine fork. (Do not overmix.)

2. Shape meat into rectangle, 10x16, on waxed paper or aluminum foil.

3. Spread BREAD AND BUTTER STUFFING in an even layer over meat.

4. Roll up meat, jelly-roll fashion. (To roll meat easily, lift paper or foil with left hand and guide meat with right hand as it forms a roll; continue until meat is completely rolled.)

5. Place roll, seam side down, in shallow baking pan; mark top lightly into squares with knife.

6. Bake in moderate oven (350°F) 1 hour, or until meat is cooked the way you like it.

7. Lift roll with 2 pancake turners onto heated platter. Garnish top with onion rings, if desired.

TEXAS MEAT BALLS

Texas Meat Balls

Makes 4 servings

  1 package (4 ounces) corn
    chips, crushed
  1 pound ground beef
  1 small onion, finely chopped (¼ cup)
  ¼ cup chopped parsley
  1 egg, unbeaten
  ½ teaspoon salt
  ¼ teaspoon marjoram
  Fat for frying

1. Place ½ package corn chips in shallow dish or pie plate; save for Step 3.

2. Combine beef, remaining corn chips, onion, parsley, egg, salt, and marjoram in medium-size bowl; toss together lightly with 2-tine fork. (Do not overmix.)

3. Shape into 24 small balls; roll in crushed corn chips in pie plate.

4. Fry meat balls over medium heat in hot fat in medium-size frying pan 5 minutes, or until meat is brown and cooked the way you like it. Serve with chili sauce or catsup, if desired.

Rice and Beef Porcupines

Makes 6 servings

1½ pounds ground beef
¼ cup raw rice
1 large onion, finely chopped (1 cup)
1 tablespoon Worcestershire sauce
1½ teaspoons salt (for meat)
⅛ teaspoon pepper
  Fat for frying
2 cans condensed tomato soup
1 can water (measured in soup can)
1 clove of garlic, minced
1 bay leaf
1 teaspoon salt (for sauce)
¼ teaspoon thyme
4 carrots, scraped and cut into bite-size
  pieces
4 medium-size potatoes, pared and cut
  into bite-size pieces
12 small white onions (about ½ pound),
  peeled
1 package quick-frozen green peas
1 package quick-frozen whole-kernel
  corn

1. Combine beef, rice, onion, Worcestershire sauce, salt (for meat), and pepper in medium-size bowl; toss together with fork. (Do not overmix.)
2. Shape into 12 balls.
3. Brown meat balls over medium heat in hot fat in large heavy kettle with tight-fitting cover, or Dutch oven; remove balls; drain on absorbent paper; save for Step 6; pour any remaining fat from kettle.
4. Blend tomato soup, water, garlic, bay leaf, salt (for sauce), and thyme in same kettle; bring to boiling.
5. Add carrots, potatoes, and onions; cover tightly; reduce heat; simmer 15 minutes.
6. Place meat balls on top of vegetables in kettle; baste with sauce; cover.
7. Simmer 30 minutes, or until vegetables are tender. If needed, stir stew

Left—RICE AND BEEF PORCUPINES

very gently after 15 minutes to keep vegetables from sticking.
8. Cook peas and corn in boiling salted water following directions on packages while stew cooks; drain; season to taste with salt, pepper, and butter or margarine; keep hot.
9. Pour stew into heated serving dish; spoon hot peas and corn around edge.

Meat-Ball Goulash with Spaghetti

Makes 6 servings

1 pound ground beef
1 medium-size onion, chopped (½ cup)
½ cup (about 1 slice) coarse bread
  crumbs
1 egg, unbeaten
1 teaspoon salt (for meat)
¼ teaspoon thyme
¼ teaspoon pepper
2 tablespoons fat
3 cups water
1 can condensed cream of mushroom
  soup
1 can (8 ounces) tomato sauce
1½ teaspoons salt (for sauce)
½ bay leaf
1 package (8 ounces) thin spaghetti,
  broken into 2-inch lengths

1. Combine beef, ¼ cup of onion, bread crumbs, egg, salt (for meat), thyme, and pepper in medium-size bowl; toss together lightly with 2-tine fork. (Do not overmix.)
2. Shape into 30 small balls.
3. Brown meat balls over medium heat in hot fat in large heavy frying pan with tight-fitting cover.
4. Stir in water, soup, tomato sauce, remaining onion, salt (for sauce), and bay leaf; bring mixture to boiling; add spaghetti; cover tightly.
5. Simmer 25 to 30 minutes, or until spaghetti is tender, stirring occasionally to keep spaghetti from sticking.

Meat Balls in Tomato Sauce

Makes 6 servings

1½ pounds ground beef
  1 medium-size onion, finely chopped
    (½ cup)
  ⅓ cup chopped parsley
  1 egg, unbeaten
  ½ cup (about 1 slice) soft bread crumbs
  ¾ teaspoon salt
  ¼ teaspoon marjoram
    Dash of pepper
    Tomato Sauce, page 130
    Boiled rice or noodles

1. Combine beef, onion, parsley, egg, bread crumbs, salt, marjoram, and pepper in medium-size bowl; toss together lightly with 2-tine fork. (Do not overmix.)
2. Shape into bite-size balls; drop each into hot TOMATO SAUCE.
3. Simmer, stirring once or twice, 5 minutes, or just until cooked the way you like them.
4. Serve meat balls in sauce with boiled rice or noodles.

Frosted Meat Loaf

Bake at 350°F about 1 hour, 20 minutes . . . Makes 6 servings

1½ pounds ground beef
  1 small onion, finely chopped (¼ cup)
  ½ cup (about 1 slice) coarse bread
    crumbs
  ½ cup milk
  1 teaspoon Worcestershire sauce
  1 egg, unbeaten
1½ teaspoons salt
  ⅛ teaspoon pepper
  5 cups hot seasoned mashed potatoes
    (about 6 medium size)

1. Combine beef, onion, bread crumbs, milk, Worcestershire sauce, egg, salt, and pepper in medium-size bowl; toss together lightly with 2-tine fork. (Do not overmix.)
2. Pack mixture into loaf pan, 9x5x3; spread evenly.
3. Bake in moderate oven (350°F) 1 hour, or until meat is cooked the way you like it.
4. Place loaf on shallow baking pan; leave oven heat on.
5. Frost top and sides of loaf with hot mashed potatoes, leaving ends of loaf unfrosted.
6. Return loaf to oven; bake 20 minutes, or until peaks of potatoes are lightly browned.
7. Place loaf on heated platter; garnish with sliced tomatoes and parsley, if desired.

Meat-Loaf Shortcake

Bake at 350°F for 25 to 30 minutes . . . Makes 6 to 8 servings

  1 pound ground beef
  ½ pound ground veal
  ½ pound ground pork
  1 cup (about 2 slices) soft bread crumbs
  1 cup catsup
  ¾ cup milk
  1 egg, slightly beaten
  1 large onion, chopped (1 cup)
  2 teaspoons Worcestershire sauce
1½ teaspoons salt
  ¼ teaspoon pepper
    Dash of cayenne
  4 cups hot seasoned mashed potatoes
    (about 5 medium-size)
    Mushroom Sauce, page 131

1. Combine beef, veal, pork, bread crumbs, catsup, milk, egg, onion, Worcestershire sauce, and seasonings in large bowl; toss together lightly with 2-tine fork. (Do not overmix.)
2. Divide mixture in half; pat lightly into 2 eight-inch layer-cake pans.
3. Bake in moderate oven (350°F) 25 to 30 minutes, or until meat is cooked the way you like it.

To cut meat-loaf baking time in half, spoon mixture into large muffin-pan cups.

4. Place 1 meat layer, using pancake turner or large spatula, on heated platter; cover with hot mashed potatoes; spread evenly; top with second meat layer; serve with MUSHROOM SAUCE.

Little Hamburger Pies

Bake at 450°F about 20 minutes . . .
Makes 5 servings

  4 carrots, scraped and cut into bite-size pieces
18 small white onions, peeled (about ¾ pound)
  4 medium-size potatoes, pared and cut into bite-size pieces
  1 medium-size yellow onion, finely chopped (½ cup)
  2 tablespoons fat
  1 pound ground beef
  1 can condensed tomato soup
  1 cup water
  2 teaspoons salt
⅛ teaspoon pepper
  1 package piecrust mix

1. Cook carrots, onions, and potatoes, covered, in 2 inches boiling salted water in large saucepan 20 minutes, or just until tender; drain; return to saucepan.
2. Saute yellow onion in hot fat in medium-size frying pan over low heat 5 minutes, or just until tender; add beef; brown over medium heat, breaking up meat with 2-tine fork as it cooks.
3. Stir soup, water, salt, and pepper into meat mixture; bring to boiling; reduce heat; simmer 5 minutes; add to vegetables; keep hot.
4. Prepare pastry according to directions on package of mix.
5. Roll out dough ⅛ inch thick on lightly floured pastry cloth or board; mark 5 pastry circles with rim of an individual casserole (2-cup size); cut out circles with pastry wheel or sharp-pointed knife.
6. Cut large cross in center of each round; fold points over to rim of circle to make square opening in center.
7. Fill 5 individual casseroles with hot meat mixture; top with pastry rounds.
8. Bake in hot oven (450° F) 20 minutes, or until pastry is golden-brown.

Old-Fashioned Meat Loaf

Bake at 350°F about 1 hour . . .
Makes 6 servings

1½ pounds ground beef
  1 small onion, finely chopped (¼ cup)
½ cup (about 1 slice) soft bread crumbs
⅓ cup milk
⅓ cup chili sauce
  1 egg, unbeaten
1½ teaspoons salt
⅛ teaspoon pepper

1. Combine all ingredients in medium-size bowl; toss together lightly with 2-tine fork. (Do not overmix.)
2. Pack mixture in loaf pan, 9x5x3; level top.
3. Bake in moderate oven (350°F) 1 hour, or until meat is cooked the way you like it.
4. Place on heated platter; garnish with onion rings and additional chili sauce, if desired.

29

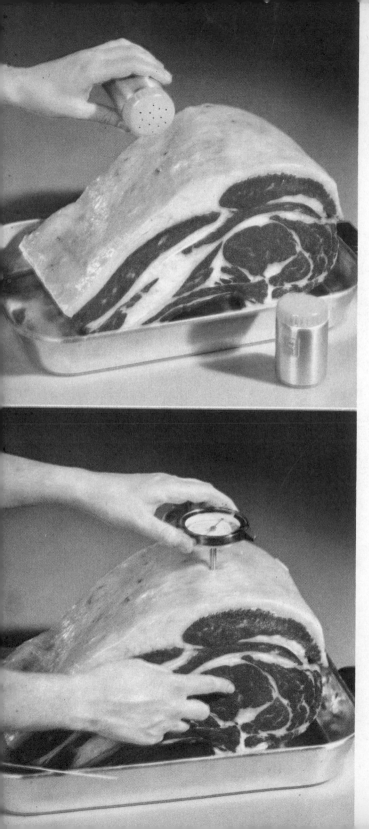

How to Roast Prime Ribs

Stand roast in pan fat side up, so melting top layer bastes meat as it cooks. Use no rack — low roasting temperature won't overbrown meat on bottom or make it stick to pan. Rub surface with cut garlic and sprinkle with salt and pepper, or use your favorite seasoning salt. Don't add water or cover pan during roasting. Don't baste meat.

Use a meat thermometer to tell when roast is cooked just right. Insert it so tip comes to center part of roast without touching fat or bone. Measure distance first on outside of roast; then make a hole for thermometer with skewer or knife. No thermometer? Then follow the TIMETABLE, page 34.

and Carve
of Beef

CARVE: *Let meat stand about 5 minutes after it comes from oven so it's easier to slice. Place it flat, "eye" up, on heated platter. Go light on garnishes. Place platter with rib side of roast to carver's left, rib ends towards him. Carver holds roast with fork below top rib and slices meat from the outside in toward the ribs.*

Cut close to ribs with point of knife to release the slices from bones. Serve each slice neatly and surely by lifting on flat of knife blade, steadying with fork. A good sharp knife is carver's best friend —and the thinner the blade, the better. Slice with long smooth even strokes. No sawing, please!

| Standing rib roast | Rolled rib roast | Rolled rump roast |

Beef Roasts

To Buy *Standing rib, rolled rib, top sirloin,* and *beef tenderloin* are sold for dry-heat cooking or roasting. *Rump, chuck* (rib or blade-bone shoulder), *shoulder arm, heel of round, sirloin-tip,* and *English-* or *Boston-cut* are sold for moist cooking or pot roasting.

STANDING RIB ROASTS These are the most expensive, but the tenderest of the beef roasts. Buy one when you are planning a family party and want something especially nice. A rib roast should be at least 2 ribs thick or 4 pounds in weight. The choicest cut is made up of the 11th and 12th ribs (also known as "first" ribs). Next in quality and tenderness are the 8th to the 10th ribs. Least desirable but less expensive because they are less tender are the 6th and 7th ribs. *Blade rib roasts,* cut from the heavy end of the rib, are more economical but not so tender. In many stores the short rib ends are removed and the roast is sold as a 7-inch cut. The backbone and gristle are also cut out and the meat is covered with a thin layer of fat for even cooking. If the roast is not prepared this way, have it fixed "hotel" style. For easy serving, the meatman cuts the backbone so it can be removed easily after cooking.

ROLLED RIB ROASTS These are made by boning standing rib roasts. They are more difficult to carve because of the strings needed to hold them together. If you buy a rolled roast, be certain that it does not contain the rib ends. Buy ¼ pound, boned, per serving.

SIRLOIN TIP This is a boneless, easily carved roast sold extensively in most parts of the United States. Roast may be rolled and tied. Roast only the best grades, pot roast the lower grades. Allow ¼ pound per serving.

BEEF TENDERLOIN This is the tenderest and most expensive of all beef cuts and makes a wonderful company roast. The tenderloins of low-grade beef are often sold for roasting. The tenderloin is also sliced into steaks and sold as *filet mignon.* Allow ½ to 1 pound, untrimmed, per serving.

RUMP This makes a flavorful and economical pot roast. Use either a bone-in or boneless rolled roast. Pot roasts should be at least 2 inches thick. Allow ⅓ pound, bone-in, or ¼ pound, boned, per serving.

CHUCK This pot roast is rich in flavor, economical, and tender. The center cuts generally known as "seven bone" are more desirable than cuts taken from the *rib end* or those lying next to the neck. Allow ⅓ pound, bone-in, or ¼ pound, boned, per serving.

SHOULDER ARM This is an economical, lean, rich-flavored cut that comes from the lower part of the chuck. Better grades make excellent pot roast, lower

| Inside chuck pot roast | Arm pot roast | English- or Boston-cut roast |

grades should be stewed. Allow ⅓ pound, bone-in, or ¼ pound, boned, per serving.

HEEL OF ROUND This is a boneless, lean, triangular-shaped piece from the lower part of the round. It is flavorful but tough and requires long moist cooking. Better grades are pot roasted, lower grades are stewed or ground. Allow ¼ pound per serving.

"ENGLISH-" or "BOSTON-"CUT This contains the rib ends of the first chuck ribs or may be taken from the arm by omitting the round bone portion of the roast. It is usually sold boneless. It is a flavorful but less tender cut that must be braised. Allow ⅓ pound, bone-in, or ¼ pound, boned, per serving.

To Store Wrap roast loosely in waxed paper or aluminum foil. Store in your refrigerator. Cook within 7 days.

Standing Rib Roast of Beef

1. Buy 2 to 3 ribs of beef weighing 5½ to 8 pounds.*
2. Place on rack, fat side up, in open roasting pan; insert meat thermometer so bulb reaches center of cut. (If you do not have a thermometer, weigh roast, then figure time needed using TIME-TABLE, page 34.) (See photographs, page 30.)

*To figure number of servings, allow ½ pound, bone-in, per person. It is seldom wise to buy less than a 4-pound roast, as shrinkage is proportionately higher in a small roast.

3. Do not add water. Do not cover pan.
4. Roast beef in slow oven (325°F), for time needed, depending on its weight, or until meat thermometer registers degree of doneness you like.
5. Place on heated platter; let meat stand about 15 minutes to make it easier to carve; garnish with parsley or water cress, if desired.
6. Make gravy following directions, page 132 or 133, if desired.

Rolled Rib Roast

5 pounds rib roast of beef, boned and rolled
Yorkshire Pudding, page 134
Parsley

1. Place meat on rack, fat side up, in open roasting pan; insert meat thermometer so bulb reaches center of cut. (If you do not have a thermometer, figure time needed using TIMETABLE, page 34.)
2. Do not add water. Do not cover pan.
3. Roast beef in slow oven (325°F) for time needed, or until meat thermometer registers degree of doneness you like.
4. Place roast on heated platter; keep hot.
5. Make YORKSHIRE PUDDING.
6. Place pudding squares around roast; garnish with parsley.

TIMETABLE*

Beef Roasts†

	Oven Temp.	Degree of Doneness	Minutes per lb.	Meat Thermometer
Standing Rib Roast	325°F	Rare	18-22	140°F
(5-6 pounds)		Medium	23-28	160°F
		Well done	27-33	170°F
Standing Rib Roast	325°F	Rare	17-19	140°F
(7-8 pounds)		Medium	20-23	160°F
		Well done	25-29	170°F
Rolled Rib Roast	325°F	Rare	27-33	140°F
		Medium	32-39	160°F
		Well done	37-44	170°F
Beef Tenderloin Roast	425°F	Rare	12-15	140°F
Sirloin Tip	325°F	Rare	20-24	140°F
(about 4 pounds)		Medium	30-34	160°F
(top grades)		Well done	44-48	170°F

*The amount of bone, thickness of cut, and many other factors affect roasting time. Roast your meat the way you like it using these figures as guides.

†Time is for chilled meat from the refrigerator.

Beef Tenderloin Roast

1. Buy whole beef tenderloin* (will weigh 2 to 4 pounds, trimmed). Have roast trimmed and larded.
2. Place on rack, larded side up, in open roasting pan; insert meat thermometer so bulb reaches center of cut. (If you do not have a thermometer, weigh roast, then figure the time needed using TIMETABLE, above.)
3. Do not add water. Do not cover pan.
4. Roast tenderloin in hot oven (425°F)† for time needed, or until meat thermometer registers 140°F. (Roasted beef tenderloin should be crusty brown on the outside and rare or almost rare on the inside.) Remove roast from oven.
5. Place meat on heated platter; serve with THIN PAN GRAVY, page 132, or MADEIRA-MUSHROOM SAUCE, page 129.

*Excellent for a company roast. Buy either lower quality grades or top quality tenderloin; have roast trimmed and larded.
†This is an exception to the low-temperature rule.

Pot Roast of Beef

4 pounds pot roast (chuck, round, or rump)
Seasoned Flour, page 41
3 tablespoons fat
2 tablespoons prepared mustard
2 large onions, sliced
1 bay leaf
1½ cups water
1 teaspoon salt
½ teaspoon pepper

1. Rub meat well with SEASONED FLOUR; brown over medium heat on all sides in hot fat in large heavy frying pan with tight-fitting cover, or Dutch oven; pour off any excess fat.

2. Spread top of beef with mustard; add onions, bay leaf, water, salt, and pepper; cover tightly.

3. Bring to boiling; reduce heat; simmer 1½ to 2½ hours, or until meat is tender when pierced with 2-tine fork.

Or bake meat, covered, in very slow oven (300°F) about 2 hours.

4. Place meat on platter; keep hot.

5. Make gravy following directions, page 133.

Sauerbraten

    2 cups vinegar
    2 cups water
    3 bay leaves
 10 peppercorns
    1 teaspoon whole cloves
    1 medium-size onion, sliced
    4 pounds pot roast
2½ tablespoons **Seasoned Flour,**
        page 41
    2 tablespoons fat
    6 carrots, scraped and quartered
    6 medium-size onions, peeled
        Potato Pancakes, page 136

1. Combine vinegar, water, bay leaves, peppercorns, cloves, and sliced onion in medium-size saucepan; bring to boiling.

2. Place meat in large bowl; pour hot vinegar mixture over meat; cover bowl; marinate 2 days in refrigerator, turning meat several times.

3. Remove meat; drain; rub well with SEASONED FLOUR; brown on all sides over medium heat in hot fat in large heavy kettle with tight-fitting cover, or Dutch oven; add marinade liquid to depth of ½ inch (about 1½ cups); cover tightly.

4. Bring to boiling; reduce heat; simmer 2½ hours.

5. Remove cover; arrange carrots and peeled onions around meat; cover; simmer 1 hour, or until meat and vegetables are cooked the way you like them.

6. Place meat and vegetables on heated platter; keep hot.

7. MAKE GRAVY: Skim any excess fat from liquid in pan; measure, adding water if needed to make 2 cups; return to pan. Stir in 1 tablespoon sugar, ½ teaspoon salt, and 6 tablespoons gingersnap crumbs (about 8 small gingersnaps); cook over low heat, stirring constantly, until gravy thickens.

8. Slice SAUERBRATEN; serve with accompanying vegetables, gravy, and POTATO PANCAKES.

Cranberry Roast

    4 pounds rump, boned and rolled
        Seasoned Flour, page 41
    1 clove of garlic, cut
        Handful of celery tops
 ½ cup water
 ¼ cup orange juice
    1 cup fresh cranberries
    2 tablespoons sugar
1½ teaspoons salt
 ¼ teaspoon pepper
 ½ teaspoon Worcestershire sauce

1. Rub meat well with SEASONED FLOUR; brown on all sides over medium heat in Dutch oven first rubbed with cut garlic.

2. Add garlic, celery tops, water, orange juice, cranberries, sugar, salt, pepper, and Worcestershire sauce; cover tightly.

3. Bring to boiling; reduce heat; simmer 2 to 2½ hours, or until meat is tender when pierced with 2-tine fork.

4. Place meat on platter; keep hot.

5. Make gravy following directions, page 133.

CRANBERRY ROAST

Italian Pot Roast

4 pounds pot roast (chuck, round, or rump)
1 tablespoon olive oil
3 large onions, sliced
2 cloves of garlic, speared with wooden picks
1½ teaspoons salt
½ teaspoon marjoram
½ teaspoon thyme
¼ teaspoon pepper
½ cup water
1 can (6 ounces) tomato paste

1. Brown meat on all sides over medium heat in hot olive oil in large heavy kettle with tight-fitting cover.
2. Add onions, garlic, salt, marjoram, thyme, pepper, water, and ½ can of tomato paste (save rest for Step 5); cover tightly.
3. Bring to boiling; reduce heat; simmer 2 to 2½ hours, or until meat is tender when pierced with 2-tine fork. (Add water during cooking, if needed.)
4. Place meat on platter; keep hot.
5. Make gravy following directions, page 133; add remaining tomato paste.

Pressure-Cooker Pot Roast

5 pounds pot roast (chuck or rump)
Seasoned Flour, page 41
2 tablespoons fat
¼ cup water
¼ cup vinegar
4 whole cloves
1 bay leaf
6 medium-size potatoes, pared and cut in halves
6 medium-size onions, peeled
6 carrots, scraped and quartered

1. Rub meat well with SEASONED FLOUR; brown on all sides over medium heat in hot fat in 6- or 7-quart pressure cooker.
2. Slip trivet under meat in cooker; add water, vinegar, cloves, and bay leaf.
3. Cover cooker; cook at 15 pounds pressure for 1 hour and 20 minutes.
4. Cool cooker quickly, according to manufacturer's directions; remove cover.
5. Add potatoes, onions, and carrots.
6. Cover cooker; cook at 15 pounds pressure 10 minutes.
7. Cool cooker quickly, according to manufacturer's directions; remove cover.
8. Place roast and vegetables on heated platter; keep hot; remove trivet from cooker.
9. Make gravy following directions, page 133.

Beef Banquet

4 pounds sirloin-tip roast
Seasoned Flour, page 41
1 large onion, chopped (1 cup)
1 small green pepper, chopped
1 can (8 ounces) tomato sauce
1 teaspoon salt
¼ teaspoon pepper
1 package (8 ounces) macaroni
Grated process American cheese

1. Rub meat well with SEASONED FLOUR; brown on all sides over medium heat in Dutch oven.
2. Add onion, green pepper, tomato sauce, salt, and pepper; cover tightly.
3. Bring to boiling; reduce heat; simmer 2 to 2½ hours, or until meat is tender when pierced with 2-tine fork. (Add water during cooking, if needed, to keep about 1 cup liquid in Dutch oven.)
4. Cook macaroni according to directions on package ½ hour before meat is done; drain.
5. Place meat on heated platter; keep hot.
6. Skim any excess fat from liquid in Dutch oven; stir in macaroni; simmer 3 to 4 minutes; spoon macaroni and sauce around meat; sprinkle macaroni with grated cheese.

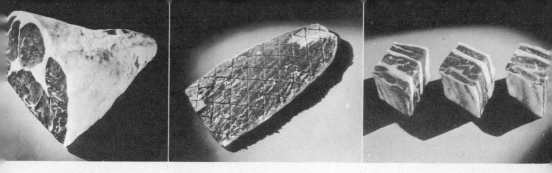

Heel of round   Flank steak   Short ribs

Other Cuts of Beef

Meat cut from the *round, rump, sirloin,* and *chuck; flank steak;* and *short ribs* are used for braising. *Round, neck, shank, plate,* and *brisket* (fresh or corned) are stewed (cooked covered with water or other liquid).

ROUND Depending upon the grade, round can be broiled or pan-fried (Prime only), roasted (Prime only), braised, or stewed (all the other grades). In parts of the United States, the round is divided into *top, bottom,* and *heel.* Of these the top is the most tender. The bottom is sometimes cubed to make it more tender, is used for Swiss steak, or is ground. If the round is not cut into these three parts, and your family is small, separate them at home. Broil or pan-fry the top, "Swiss" the bottom, and use the heel for a small stew.

RUMP Prime or Choice grades can be roasted, other grades are better braised.

SIRLOIN This is generally cut into steaks, but the bottom sirloin and sirloin tip, less tender than top, are also braised.

CHUCK This is one of the most versatile of beef cuts. Top grades (Prime and Choice) can be broiled (with the aid of tenderizers), pan-fried, or roasted. Other grades are braised or stewed.

FLANK Very lean and boneless, this is a less tender and economical steak. It is about 1 inch thick, 12 to 14 inches long, 4 to 6 inches wide and weighs about 1½ pounds. There are only 2 steaks on each carcass. The fibers run lengthwise, so flank steaks are usually sliced at an angle across the fibers.

SHORT RIBS These are cut from the ends of rib roast. They are usually cut into 2-inch squares weighing 4 to 6 ounces each. Those from the best grades of beef are fatty. Buy 1 to 2 pieces per serving.

NECK and SHANK These must be stewed, ground, or "boiled," and need long cooking to make them tender. Both are very lean and inexpensive. Shank is coarse but flavorful. It is sold boned or bone-in and is used for stew or soup. Soup bones generally are priced according to amount of meat on them.

PLATE and BRISKET These contain a high percentage of bone and, in well-finished beef, a large amount of fat. They are boned and rolled often for stewing or are cured and sold as *corned beef.*

CORNED BEEF When of good quality this is not too fatty (should have 3 parts meat, 1 part fat). The thicker half of a corned brisket will weigh 4 to 6½ pounds. A whole brisket is a wedge-shaped piece varying in thickness from 2 inches at one end to 5 at the other.

Beef Ragout with Parsley-Chives Dumplings

Makes 6 servings

2½ pounds boneless brisket, rump, or chuck, cut into 1-inch cubes
¼ cup **Seasoned Flour**, page 41
3 tablespoons fat
2 cloves of garlic, minced
2¼ cups (1-pint, 2-ounce can) tomato juice
2 bay leaves
3 whole cloves
1 tablespoon sugar
1 teaspoon salt
½ teaspoon marjoram
¼ teaspoon pepper
Few sprigs of parsley
12 small white onions, peeled (about ½ pound)
1 bunch small carrots, scraped and halved
Parsley-Chives Dumplings, page 134
1 can (about 1 pound) peas, heated

1. Dust meat cubes well with SEASONED FLOUR placed in a paper bag.

2. Heat fat with garlic in large heavy frying pan with tight-fitting cover, or in Dutch oven; brown meat, a few pieces at a time, over medium heat; drain on absorbent paper; pour off any excess fat.

3. Return meat to pan; add tomato juice, bay leaves, cloves, sugar, salt, marjoram, pepper, and parsley; cover tightly.

4. Bring to boiling; reduce heat; simmer about 1 hour.

5. Add onions and carrots; cover; simmer 1 hour, or until meat and vegetables are tender when pierced with 2-tine fork.

6. Twenty minutes before serving, spoon PARSLEY-CHIVES DUMPLINGS mixture on top of steaming-hot ragout; cook, uncovered, 10 minutes; cover; steam 10 minutes longer.

7. Spoon ragout into heated serving dish; add heated peas; arrange dumplings around edge.

Philadelphia Beef Stew

Makes 6 servings

2 pounds boneless chuck, shank, or round, cut into 1-inch cubes
¼ cup flour
3 tablespoons fat
1 can (8 ounces) tomato sauce
3 cups boiling water
1 medium-size onion, chopped (½ cup)
1 clove of garlic, minced
2 whole cloves
½ bay leaf
2 teaspoons salt
¼ teaspoon pepper
6 potatoes, peeled and quartered
6 carrots, scraped and cut into 1-inch pieces
12 small white onions, peeled (about ½ pound)
1 cup cooked peas

1. Dust meat cubes well with flour placed in a paper bag.

2. Brown meat on all sides over medium heat in hot fat in large heavy frying pan with tight-fitting cover, or Dutch oven; drain on absorbent paper; pour off any remaining fat.

3. Return meat to pan; add tomato sauce, boiling water, onion, garlic, cloves, bay leaf, salt, and pepper; cover tightly.

4. Bring to boiling; reduce heat; simmer 1 to 1½ hours, or until meat is tender when pierced with 2-tine fork; add potatoes, carrots, and onions; cover.

5. Simmer 20 minutes, or until vegetables are tender when pierced with 2-tine fork; stir in peas.

6. Serve piping hot.

Right—PHILADELPHIA BEEF STEW

Hungarian Goulash

Makes 4 servings

3 large onions, thinly sliced
3 tablespoons fat
1¼ pounds boneless chuck or round, cut into 1-inch cubes
3 teaspoons paprika
1 teaspoon salt
⅛ teaspoon pepper
Dash of cayenne
1 bay leaf
½ cup water
1 cup sour cream
Egg Dumplings, page 135

1. Saute onions in hot fat in large heavy frying pan with tight-fitting cover over low heat 10 to 15 minutes, or just until tender; remove; save for Step 3.
2. Brown meat over medium heat in remaining fat.
3. Add paprika, salt, pepper, cayenne, onions, bay leaf, and water; cover tightly.
4. Bring to boiling; reduce heat; simmer, stirring occasionally, 50 to 60 minutes, or until meat is tender when pierced with 2-tine fork.
5. Remove from heat; fold in sour cream. Serve immediately with EGG DUMPLINGS.

Beef Strogonoff

Makes 6 servings

2 pounds round steak, cut ¾-inch thick
2 tablespoons fat
2 teaspoons dry mustard
1 teaspoon salt
⅛ teaspoon pepper
2 cups water
1 cup sour cream

1. Cut meat in long, narrow strips; brown on all sides over medium heat in hot fat in large heavy frying pan with tight-fitting cover, or Dutch oven.

BEEF STROGONOFF

2. Blend in mustard, salt, and pepper; stir in water; cover tightly.
3. Bring to boiling; reduce heat; simmer, stirring occasionally, 1 hour, or until meat is tender when pierced with 2-tine fork.
4. Make gravy following directions, page 133.
5. Return meat to gravy; stir in sour cream; simmer, stirring constantly, just until hot. (Do not boil mixture or cream will curdle.) Serve in ring of hot mashed potatoes, if desired.

Swiss Steak with Noodles

Makes 4 to 6 servings

2 pounds round or rump steak, cut 2 inches thick
3 tablespoons **Seasoned Flour,** page 41
1 large onion, chopped (1 cup)
1 green pepper, chopped
2 cups (about 1-pound can) tomatoes
1½ teaspoons salt
Buttered noodles
Onion rings

1. Rub steak well with SEASONED FLOUR; pound well into steak.
2. Rub heavy frying pan with tight-fitting cover with piece of fat cut from edge of steak; brown steak on both sides over medium heat.
3. Add onion, green pepper, tomatoes, and salt; cover tightly.

4. Bring to boiling; reduce heat; simmer 1½ to 2 hours, or until steak is tender when pierced with 2-tine fork.
5. Place steak on heated platter; keep hot.
6. Make gravy following directions, page 133.
7. Serve steak with buttered noodles; garnish with onion rings.

Burgundy Beef

Makes 4 servings

    1 medium-size onion, sliced
    1 bay leaf
    ¼ teaspoon rosemary
    1 cup Burgundy wine
    1 tablespoon vinegar
    1 tablespoon salad oil
1½ pounds rump steak, ½-inch thick,
        cut into 2-inch pieces
    ¼ pound salt pork, finely diced
    ½ pound small mushrooms
    1 beef-bouillon cube, dissolved in
        ¾ cup hot water
    2 tablespoons flour
    ¼ cup water

1. Combine onion, bay leaf, rosemary, wine, vinegar, and salad oil in large bowl; add meat; marinate 1 hour, turning meat occasionally. (Liquid should cover meat.)
2. Drain; save liquid for Step 4.
3. Fry salt pork over medium heat in Dutch oven; add mushrooms and meat-onion mixture; cook until onion is tender.
4. Stir in bouillon and marinade; cover tightly.
5. Bring to boiling; reduce heat; simmer 1 hour; remove cover; simmer 30 minutes.
6. Blend flour to smooth paste with water in cup; stir into meat mixture slowly.
7. Cook over low heat, stirring constantly, until mixture thickens and boils 1 minute.

Pepper Steak

Makes 4 to 6 servings

    1 flank steak (about 1½ pounds), cut
        into ¼-inch strips
    1 chicken-bouillon cube, dissolved in
        ½ cup hot water
    1 clove of garlic
    3 tablespoons soy sauce
    1 large onion, finely chopped (1 cup)
    1 can (3 or 4 ounces) sliced mushrooms
    1 tablespoon sugar
    ⅛ teaspoon pepper
    1 tablespoon flour
    2 tablespoons water
    2 green peppers, cut into *thin* strips

1. Brown fatty pieces of steak over medium heat in large heavy frying pan with tight-fitting cover, or Dutch oven; push to side of pan.
2. Brown remaining steak strips on all sides; remove all steak from pan; save for Step 5.
3. Pour bouillon into frying pan; add garlic; simmer 3 to 4 minutes; remove garlic.
4. Stir in soy sauce, onion, mushrooms, sugar, and pepper.
5. Blend flour to smooth paste with water in cup; stir into onion mixture; add browned meat; cover tightly.
6. Simmer, stirring occasionally, 20 minutes, or until meat is tender when pierced with 2-tine fork.
7. Add green peppers; cover; simmer 10 minutes. Serve with buttered noodles or rice, if desired.

Seasoned Flour*

Makes 1 cup

    1 cup flour
    2 teaspoons salt
    ¼ teaspoon pepper

1. Measure flour, salt, and pepper into sifter; sift into small bowl; blend thoroughly.
2. Place in small jar; cover.

Keep this on hand; use for thickening (gravies, sauces, and stews) and coating or dusting meat.

Sukiyaki

Makes 4 servings

¾ pound round steak, cut 1 inch thick
½ pound mushrooms, thinly sliced
1 bunch green onions, cut in 1½-inch
   lengths
3 stalks celery, sliced
2 large yellow onions, thinly sliced
1 can (8 ounces) bamboo shoots, drained
3 tablespoons sugar
⅓ cup soy sauce
1 chicken-bouillon cube, dissolved in
   ½ cup hot water
3 cups raw spinach leaves
3 cups cooked rice (about ¾ cup raw)

1. Cut round steak diagonally across the grain into very thin slices.
2. Rub heavy frying pan with piece of fat cut from edge of steak; brown meat on both sides over medium heat.
3. Add all ingredients except spinach and rice.
4. Simmer, stirring often, 10 minutes, or until vegetables are just tender.
5. Add spinach; cook 5 minutes. (Vegetables should be crisply tender.)
6. Arrange rice in ring on heated serving platter; fill with SUKIYAKI.

Stuffed Beef Rolls

Makes 6 servings

6 cube steaks
   Salt and pepper
2½ cups ready-mix bread stuffing
¾ cup water
2 tablespoons melted butter or
   margarine
2 tablespoons fat
1 clove of garlic, minced
1 can (8 ounces) tomato sauce
⅛ teaspoon ground cloves

1. Sprinkle steaks with salt and pepper to taste.
2. Combine bread stuffing, water, and melted butter or margarine in medium-size bowl; toss together lightly with 2-tine fork.
3. Spread stuffing thinly on each steak; roll up; fasten with skewers or tie with clean white string.
4. Heat fat with garlic in large heavy frying pan with tight-fitting cover, or Dutch oven; brown beef rolls, a few at a time, on all sides, over medium heat; pour off excess fat; returns rolls to pan.
5. Add tomato sauce and cloves; cover tightly.
6. Bring to boiling; reduce heat; simmer 1 hour, or until rolls are tender when pierced with 2-tine fork.
7. Arrange rolls on heated serving dish. Serve pan gravy separately.

Barbecued Minute Steaks

Makes 4 servings

4 minute or cube steaks
   Salt and pepper
1 tablespoon fat
2 cups (about 1-pound can) tomatoes
1 medium-size onion, chopped (½ cup)
½ green pepper, chopped
1 tablespoon sugar
½ teaspoon dry mustard
½ teaspoon chili powder
2 tablespoons vinegar
1 teaspoon Worcestershire sauce
4 ounces (half an 8-ounce package)
   spaghetti

1. Sprinkle steaks with salt and pepper to taste; brown on both sides over medium heat in hot fat in large heavy frying pan with tight-fitting cover; remove from pan; save for Step 3.
2. Combine tomatoes, onion, green pepper, sugar, mustard, chili powder, vinegar, and Worcestershire sauce in same frying pan; bring to boiling; reduce heat; simmer 15 minutes.
3. Return browned meat to pan; spoon sauce over it; cover tightly.

4. Simmer 30 minutes, or until meat is tender when pierced with 2-tine fork.

5. Cook spaghetti according to directions on package while meat simmers; drain; keep hot.

6. Arrange spaghetti on heated platter; place steaks on top; pour sauce over meat and spaghetti.

Flank Steak Roll (Pressure Cooker)

Makes 4 to 6 servings

1 flank steak (about 1½ pounds)
2 cups (about 4 slices) small bread cubes
1 small onion, finely chopped (¼ cup)
1 tablespoon chopped parsley
1 teaspoon salt
¼ teaspoon pepper
¼ teaspoon poultry seasoning
4 tablespoons bacon drippings
¾ cup water
½ clove of garlic

1. Score flank steak on both sides; save for Step 3.

2. Combine bread cubes, onion, parsley, salt, pepper, and poultry seasoning in medium-size bowl; sprinkle 2 tablespoons bacon drippings and 2 tablespoons water over mixture; toss together lightly with 2-tine fork.

3. Spread stuffing evenly over meat.

4. Roll up meat, jelly-roll fashion; fasten with wooden picks or metal skewers. Cut roll in half crosswise.

5. Heat remaining bacon drippings with garlic in 4-quart pressure cooker; add rolls; brown over medium heat; add remaining water.

6. Cover cooker; cook at 15 pounds pressure 40 minutes.

7. Cool cooker, according to manufacturer's directions; remove cover.

8. Place meat on heated platter; remove picks or skewers; keep hot.

9. Make gravy following directions, page 133.

Chop onions without tears with chopper available in many housewares departments.

Steak Strips in Tomato Sauce

Makes 4 to 6 servings

1 flank steak (about 1½ pounds), cut diagonally across grain into 1½-inch-wide strips
1 tablespoon fat
1 can condensed tomato soup
½ cup water
½ cup finely chopped celery
1 medium-size onion, finely chopped (½ cup)
½ teaspoon salt
⅛ teaspoon pepper

1. Brown meat on both sides over medium heat in hot fat in large heavy frying pan with tight-fitting cover; pour off excess fat.

2. Stir in tomato soup, water, celery, onion, salt, and pepper; cover tightly.

3. Bring to boiling; reduce heat; simmer 1 hour, or until meat is tender when pierced with 2-tine fork.

4. Place meat on platter; keep hot.

5. Make gravy following directions, page 133.

VARIATION

Flank Steak with Onions Substitute 1 can consomme and 2 large onions, sliced, for tomato soup, celery, and chopped onion in Step 2.

Shank cross-cuts   *Plate ribs*   *Corned brisket*

Braised Beef
Makes 4 servings

2 pounds shank, flank, chuck, or neck, cut in 1-inch cubes
1 can (8 ounces) tomato sauce
1 cup water
1 medium-size onion, chopped (½ cup)
1 clove of garlic, minced
1 teaspoon salt
½ teaspoon sugar
¼ teaspoon dry mustard
⅛ teaspoon pepper
4 cups hot seasoned mashed potatoes (about 5 medium-size)
1 tablespoon chopped parsley

1. Brown meat over medium heat in hot fat rendered from meat trimmings in large heavy frying pan with tight-fitting cover, or Dutch oven.
2. Stir in tomato sauce, water, onion, garlic, salt, sugar, mustard, and pepper; cover tightly.
3. Bring to boiling; reduce heat; simmer, stirring occasionally, 1½ to 2 hours, or until meat is tender when

pierced with 2-tine fork; skim off any excess fat.
4. Spoon hot mashed potatoes in ring on heated platter; sprinkle with parsley; spoon beef cubes and pan gravy in center of potato ring.

Steak-Potato Pan Roast
Makes 4 to 6 servings

1 flank steak (about 1½ pounds)
Seasoned Flour, page 41
2 tablespoons fat
1 tablespoon prepared mustard
1 large onion, chopped (1 cup)
Few sprigs of parsley
¾ teaspoon salt
½ cup water
¼ cup red wine
2 cups hot seasoned mashed potatoes (about 3 medium-size)
Green-pepper rings

1. Score flank steak on both sides; cut in half to make 2 steaks; rub each well with SEASONED FLOUR.
2. Brown steaks, one at a time, on both sides over medium heat in hot fat in large heavy frying pan with tight-fitting cover; pour off any excess fat.
3. Brush each steak with mustard; return to frying pan; add onion, parsley, salt, and water; cover tightly.
4. Bring to boiling; reduce heat; simmer 45 to 60 minutes, or until meat is tender when pierced with 2-tine fork. Pour wine over meat during last 15 minutes' cooking.

STEAK-POTATO PAN ROAST

5. Place one steak on heated platter; cover with mashed potatoes; top with second steak; garnish with green-pepper rings; keep hot.
6. Make gravy following directions, page 133.

Braised Short Ribs of Beef

Makes 4 to 5 servings

3 pounds short ribs of beef, cut in serving-size pieces
¼ cup **Seasoned Flour,** page 41
2 tablespoons fat
1½ cups water
1 medium-size onion, sliced

1. Rub meat well with SEASONED FLOUR; brown, a few ribs at a time, over medium heat in hot fat in large heavy frying pan with tight-fitting cover, or Dutch oven; pour off any excess fat.
2. Add water and onion; cover tightly.
3. Bring to boiling; reduce heat; simmer 1½ to 2 hours, or until meat is tender when pierced with 2-tine fork.
4. Place ribs on platter; keep hot.
5. Make gravy following directions, page 133.

Barbecued Short Ribs

Bake at 325° F for 1½ to 2 hours ...
Makes 4 servings

2½ pounds short ribs of beef, cut into serving-size pieces
1 large onion, sliced
1 cup catsup or chili sauce
½ cup vinegar
2½ teaspoons salt
1 teaspoon paprika
1 teaspoon chili powder
Dash of cayenne

1. Brown ribs, a few at a time, over medium heat in large heavy frying pan; place browned pieces in large shallow casserole with tight-fitting cover; top with onion slices.

2. Blend remaining ingredients in small bowl; pour over meat; cover tightly.
3. Bake in slow oven (325° F), basting occasionally, 1½ to 2 hours, or until meat is tender when pierced with 2-tine fork and sauce is rich and thick.

Dried Beef

To Buy Fresh chipped or dried' beef, made from the beef round, is bright red in color and moist. Buy it sliced by the pound, prepackaged, or in jars.
To Store Keep packaged dried beef in the refrigerator and tightly wrapped to prevent drying. Use within a week. Dried beef sealed in glass jars should be kept in a cool place. Use within 2 months.
To Cook If you like your dried beef salty, use it as is; if you prefer it less salty, pour boiling water over meat and drain before using it.

Creamed Dried Beef

Makes 4 servings

½ pound dried beef, shredded
¼ cup (½ stick) butter or margarine
1 medium-size onion, finely chopped (½ cup)
¼ cup flour
1 teaspoon dry mustard
2 cups milk

1. Taste beef; if very salty, pour boiling water over meat; drain well.
2. Melt butter or margarine in large heavy frying pan; saute beef and onion over low heat, stirring often with fork, 5 minutes, or until edges of beef curl.
3. Sprinkle flour and mustard over beef; mix well; slowly add milk, stirring constantly.
4. Cook over low heat, stirring constantly, until sauce thickens and boils 1 minute.
5. Serve on toast triangles, if desired.

Farm-Style Corned Beef (Pressure Cooker)

5 pounds corned-beef brisket*
3 cups water
1 medium-size head of cabbage, cut
    into 8 wedges

1. Place meat on trivet in large pressure cooker; add water.
2. Cover cooker; cook at 15 pounds pressure 1 hour and 15 minutes.
3. Cool cooker quickly, according to manufacturer's directions; remove cover; place cabbage wedges in cooker; cover; cook at 15 pounds pressure 8 minutes.
4. Cool cooker quickly; remove cover.
5. Serve meat and cabbage on heated platter with horseradish or mustard, if desired.

Brisket of Beef with Sauerkraut

Makes 4 servings

2 pounds brisket of beef
2 tablespoons fat
1 can (1 pound, 3 ounces) sauerkraut
1 medium-size onion, chopped (½ cup)
½ teaspoon salt
½ teaspoon celery salt
¼ teaspoon pepper
1 cup water
1 tablespoon caraway seeds

1. Brown meat on all sides over medium heat in hot fat in Dutch oven.
2. Add sauerkraut, onion, salt, celery salt, pepper, and water; cover tightly.
3. Bring to boiling; reduce heat; simmer 2 to 2½ hours, or until meat is tender when pierced with 2-tine fork. (Add water during cooking, if needed.)
4. Place meat on heated platter; surround with sauerkraut; sprinkle with caraway seeds.

A 5-pound brisket will serve 4 generously for 2 meals. Vegetables are planned for first meal only.

New England Boiled Dinner

5 pounds corned-beef brisket*
4 peppercorns
1 bay leaf
    Pinch of thyme
8 small potatoes, pared
12 small white onions, peeled (about
    ½ pound)
8 carrots scraped
1 small head of cabbage, cut in
    quarters
6 small beets, cooked, peeled, and
    quartered
    Or: 1 can (1 pound, 4 ounces) beets,
    quartered

1. Place meat in large heavy kettle with tight-fitting cover; add peppercorns, bay leaf, and thyme; cover with cold water.
2. Bring to boiling; skim, if needed; reduce heat; cover tightly.
3. Simmer 3½ to 4 hours, or until meat is tender when pierced with 2-tine fork.
4. Add potatoes, onions, and carrots to kettle about 45 minutes before meat is done; cook 25 minutes, then place cabbage wedges on top of vegetables; cook 20 minutes, or until vegetables are tender.
5. Heat beets in medium-size saucepan just before vegetables are done; drain.
6. Place meat on heated platter; remove vegetables from kettle and beets from saucepan with slotted spoon; drain well; arrange around meat as shown in photograph at right. Garnish top with green pepper crescents and sprinkle potatoes and onions with paprika, if desired.

Right—NEW ENGLAND BOILED DINNER

Ways with Leftover Beef...

Herb Beef Croquettes

Makes 4 servings

1½ cups ground cooked beef
  1 cup (about 2 slices) soft bread crumbs
  2 eggs, well beaten
½ teaspoon salt
½ teaspoon thyme
½ teaspoon marjoram
¼ teaspoon sage
  Few drops bottled hot-pepper sauce
⅓ cup fine dry bread crumbs
⅓ cup milk
  Melted vegetable shortening, lard, or
  salad oil to make 4-inch depth in
  kettle, or depth in electric fryer
  following manufacturer's directions

1. Combine beef, bread crumbs, eggs, salt, thyme, marjoram, sage, and bottled hot-pepper sauce in medium-size bowl; chill about 2 hours.
2. Shape into 8 croquettes; roll each in dry bread crumbs; dip in milk; roll again in dry bread crumbs; remove any loose crumbs, reshaping if needed.
3. Heat fat in deep heavy kettle to 365°F—375°F (a 1-inch cube of bread will brown in about 60 seconds); fry croquettes, 3 or 4 at a time, 2 to 3 minutes, or until golden brown; drain.
4. Serve on hot platter with WHITE SAUCE, page 128, or MUSHROOM SAUCE, page 131.

JELLIED POT ROAST

Jellied Pot Roast

Makes 4 servings

  1 envelope unflavored gelatin
½ cup cold water
  1 can consomme madrilene
  1 cup cubed cooked pot roast
½ cup cooked peas
½ cup diced cooked carrots
  6 green onions, finely chopped

1. Soften gelatin in cold water in cup.
2. Heat consomme in small saucepan; add softened gelatin, stirring until dissolved; remove from heat; chill until syrupy.
3. Arrange meat in layer in bottom of well-oiled 1-quart ring mold; spoon in enough syrupy gelatin almost to cover meat; chill until firm. (Keep remaining gelatin at room temperature.)
4. Fold peas, carrots, and onions into remaining gelatin; spoon over meat layer in mold; chill until firm.
5. Unmold onto serving dish. Serve with chili sauce, if desired.

Pennsylvania Meat Turnovers

*Bake at 350°F about 20 minutes . . .
Makes 8 turnovers*

  3 tablespoons butter or margarine
  1 large onion, finely chopped (1 cup)
½ cup finely chopped mushrooms
½ teaspoon salt
½ teaspoon oregano
  Dash of pepper
1½ cups coarsely ground cooked beef
½ cup sour cream
  Sour-Cream Pastry, page 135

1. Melt butter or margarine in medium-size frying pan; saute onion over low heat 10 to 15 minutes, or just until tender.

2. Add mushrooms, salt, oregano, pepper, and meat; heat through.

3. Remove from heat; cool slightly; stir in sour cream.

4. Cut SOUR-CREAM PASTRY into 8 rounds; divide filling evenly among rounds; fold over; pinch edges together; prick tops; place on ungreased cooky sheets.

5. Bake in moderate oven (350°F) 20 minutes, or until pastry is golden brown.

Shepherd's Pie

Bake at 450°F for 20 to 25 minutes... Makes 4 to 5 servings

 2 tablespoons butter or margarine
 2 tablespoons finely minced onion
 2 tablespoons flour
 ½ teaspoon salt
 ¼ teaspoon celery salt
 ⅛ teaspoon thyme
   Dash of pepper
 ¾ cup stock
   Or: 2 beef-bouillon cubes dissolved in ¾ cup hot water
 1½ cups diced cooked beef
 1½ cups cooked mixed vegetables
   Or: 1 package quick-frozen mixed vegetables, cooked
 1½ cups hot seasoned mashed potatoes (about 2 medium-size)

1. Melt butter or margarine in medium-size saucepan; saute onion over low heat 5 minutes, or just until tender.

2. Blend in flour, salt, celery salt, thyme, and pepper; stir in stock or bouillon gradually.

3. Cook, stirring constantly, until mixture thickens and boils 1 minute.

4. Stir in meat and vegetables; spoon mixture into greased 2-quart casserole; top with mashed potatoes.

5. Bake in hot oven (450°F) 20 to 25 minutes, or until potatoes are golden brown.

Beef Pot Pie with Pastry Topping

Bake at 425°F about 25 minutes... Makes 6 servings

 ½ cup diced celery
 1 large onion, chopped (1 cup)
 2 tablespoons chopped green pepper
 3 tablespoons fat
 3 tablespoons flour
 ¾ teaspoon salt
 ⅛ teaspoon pepper
 ⅛ teaspoon mace
   Dash of cloves
 1 cup beef stock
   Or: 2 teaspoons meat-extract paste dissolved in 1 cup hot water
 1 can (3 or 4 ounces) whole mushrooms
 1½ cups diced cooked beef
 1 teaspoon capers
 4 carrots, cooked and quartered
 1 cup cooked peas or lima beans
 ½ package piecrust mix

1. Saute celery, onion, and green pepper in hot fat in medium-size frying pan over low heat 10 to 15 minutes, or just until onion is tender.

2. Blend in flour, salt, pepper, mace, and cloves; stir in stock or meat-extract paste dissolved in hot water.

3. Cook, stirring constantly, until mixture thickens and boils 1 minute.

4. Add mushrooms, meat, capers, carrots, and peas or lima beans; keep hot.

5. Prepare pastry according to directions on package of mix; roll out to 9-inch round on floured pastry cloth or board.

6. Pour hot mixture into greased 1½-quart casserole; fit pastry over top; trim overhang to ½ inch; turn overhang under, folding flush with rim; flute edge; prick top.

7. Bake in hot oven (425°F) 25 minutes, or until pastry is golden brown.

BEEF PARMESAN

Beef Parmesan

Bake at 350°F about 25 minutes ...
Makes 4 servings

¼ cup (½ stick) butter or margarine
1 small onion, finely chopped (¼ cup)
3 tablespoons flour
1 teaspoon salt
¼ teaspoon garlic salt
⅛ teaspoon pepper
2 cups milk
½ teaspoon Worcestershire sauce
½ cup grated Parmesan cheese
1½ cups ground cooked beef
2 cups cooked spaghetti
3 tablespoons melted butter or
  margarine
3 tablespoons finely chopped parsley
3 tablespoons fine dry bread crumbs

1. Melt butter or margarine in medium-size saucepan; saute onion over low heat 5 minutes, or until tender.
2. Blend in flour, salt, garlic salt, and pepper; stir in milk gradually.
3. Cook, stirring constantly, until mixture thickens and boils 1 minute.
4. Stir in Worcestershire sauce, Parmesan cheese, and meat.
5. Arrange spaghetti and meat-cheese mixture in alternate layers in greased 1½-quart casserole.
6. Combine melted butter, parsley, and crumbs in cup; sprinkle over top.
7. Bake in moderate oven (350°F) 25 minutes, or until crumbs are brown.

Beef Menus

Cream of Tomato Soup
Pot Roast of Beef*
Paprika Potatoes   Carrots
Barbecue Aspic Mold
Cinnamon Pears
Beverage

* *

Old-Fashioned Meat Loaf*   Chili Sauce
Baked Potatoes
Swiss Spinach
Peach and Cottage Cheese Salad
Bread   Butter
Raisin Rice Pudding with Cream

* *

Grapefruit Juice
Roast Beef*
Baked Stuffed Potatoes
Peas and Onions   Corn and Pimientos
Green Salad with Blue-Cheese Dressing
Chocolate Cake
Beverage

* *

Beef Ragout with Parsley-Chives
Dumplings*
Coleslaw
Pickles   Olives   Radishes
Spiced Cherry Pie
Beverage

* *

Eggs à la Russe
Broiled Sirloin Steak*
French Fried Potatoes   Chef's Salad
Ice Cream
Beverage

*For recipes see index

50

Veal

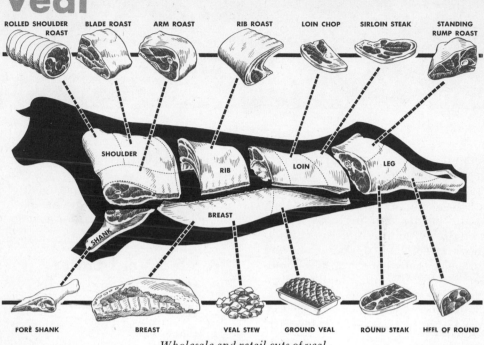

ROLLED SHOULDER ROAST   BLADE ROAST   ARM ROAST   RIB ROAST   LOIN CHOP   SIRLOIN STEAK   STANDING RUMP ROAST

SHOULDER   RIB   LOIN   LEG   BREAST   SHANK

FORE SHANK   BREAST   VEAL STEW   GROUND VEAL   ROUND STEAK   HEEL OF ROUND

Wholesale and retail cuts of veal

Veal is very young beef. The meat is delicate, tender, and juicy if well cooked. It is similar to chicken in flavor. The best veal comes from animals 4 to 14 weeks of age weighing from 40 to 100 pounds. It is most abundant in late winter and spring. In summer and fall much "veal" is really calf and more nearly resembles beef in texture and flavor.

Veal is graded according to conformation, finish, and quality. Veal animals of top grades are short and stocky with little exterior fat and no marbling. Veal is graded as U.S. Prime, U.S. Choice, U.S. Good, U.S. Commercial, U.S. Utility, and U.S. Cull, or by packers' brand names. When Government graded, veal is stamped with the grade and the word *veal* to distinguish it from *calf* which is any animal weighing 100 to 200 pounds and from 14 weeks to 1 year old. Until recently, the term veal

applied to both groups. If veal is shipped in interstate commerce it is Federally inspected and stamped, guaranteeing its wholesomeness.

Veal is grayish pink with very little fat. Any fat on top grades is firm and and creamy white. The bones show redness. The meat is very delicate in flavor.

Calf is darker in color, the bones are whiter, and there is more fat. The meat is stronger in flavor.

Very young veal, known as *bob* or *country* veal, is generally graded as Commercial or Utility. This is tasteless, watery, and considered the least desirable.

Veal, because of its lack of fat, is usually roasted, braised, or stewed. It is always cooked "well done." Roast top quality leg, rib, and loin. Small cuts from sections of the round, loin, and rib can be sauteed. Other cuts are

Round steak (cutlet)   *Sirloin steak*   *Arm steak*

better braised. Since veal has much connective tissue, slow moist cooking generally gives the best results.

Cuts of veal are similar to but much smaller in size than are those of beef. The rib and loin sections are cut into chops rather than steaks. Steaks and cutlets are cut from the sirloin, shoulder, and leg. Loin and round are high-cost cuts; shoulder, rib, rump, and shank are medium-cost; neck, fore shank, breast, and heel are low cost.

Veal Steaks and Chops

To Buy Veal *rib, sirloin,* and *shoulder* chops usually are cut ½ to 1 inch thick; the more tender loin chops are cut ¾ to 1 inch thick. Kidney chops are cut from the rib end of the loin. Loin chops are the most desirable and the most expensive. Pin-bone sirloin are the least desirable and the least expensive. Buy 1 to 2 chops per serving.

Veal *sirloin, round, arm,* and *blade* steaks usually are cut about ½ inch thick. Veal *cutlets* are individual boneless round steaks cut about ¼ inch thick and often flattened by pounding. These are the most expensive (except liver and sweetbreads) veal cuts. Arm and blade are the least expensive of the veal steaks. Buy ⅓ to ½ pound, bone-in, or ¼ to ⅓ pound, boned, per serving.

To Store Wrap loosely in waxed paper or aluminum foil; store in refrigerator; use within 5 days. If frozen, store in freezer or frozen-food compartment of your refrigerator. Cook without thawing or thaw in refrigerator or at room temperature.

Breaded Veal Cutlets
Makes 4 servings

1 egg, unbeaten
2 tablespoons milk
½ teaspoon salt
¼ teaspoon thyme
⅛ teaspoon pepper
1½ pounds veal steak, cut ½-inch thick
3 tablespoons flour
1 cup fine dry bread crumbs
3 tablespoons fat

1.   Beat egg in small bowl; stir in milk, salt, thyme, and pepper.
2.   Cut steak into 4 equal pieces; rub well with flour; dip in egg mixture; then in bread crumbs; coat thoroughly; chill ½ hour so coating will stick to meat.
3.   Brown cutlets on both sides over medium heat in hot fat in large heavy frying pan with tight-fitting cover; cover tightly.
4.   Cook over very low heat 20 to 25 minutes, or until meat is tender when pierced with 2-tine fork. (Add a small amount of water to prevent sticking, if needed.)
5.   Place cutlets on heated platter. Serve with lemon wedges or CHIVES BUTTER, page 129, if desired.

VARIATIONS

Telford Veal Cutlets Prepare BREADED VEAL CUTLETS; keep hot. Melt ¼ cup (½ stick) butter or margarine in frying pan in which cutlets were cooked. Stir in 1 can (3 or 4 ounces) sliced mushrooms, ½ teaspoon salt, and ⅛ teaspoon pepper. Blend 1 tablespoon flour to smooth paste with ½ cup stock or bouillon; add to mushroom mixture. Cook over low heat, stirring constantly, until sauce thickens and boils 1 minute. Pour mushroom sauce over cutlets; sprinkle with 2 tablespoons chopped chives.

Schnitzel Holstein Prepare BREADED VEAL CUTLETS; keep hot. Fry 4 eggs in large frying pan over low heat until whites are set. Place 1 fried egg in center of each cutlet. Garnish each cutlet with 1 or 2 anchovy fillets, if desired.

Skewered Veal

Makes 4 servings

1½ pounds veal steak, cut ¾-inch thick
¼ cup lemon juice
¼ cup salad oil
¼ cup soy sauce
⅛ teaspoon pepper
1 bay leaf, crushed

1. Cut veal into ¾-inch cubes.
2. Combine lemon juice, salad oil, soy sauce, pepper, and bay leaf in large bowl; marinate meat in lemon mixture about two hours, turning cubes occasionally.
3. Drain, saving marinade; arrange cubes on 8 six-inch skewers.
4. Broil, with top of meat 4 inches from unit or tip of flame, 20 minutes, or until tender when pierced with 2-tine fork and well browned. Baste meat with marinade and turn several times during broiling.
5. Serve on heated platter; garnish with tomato wedges, if desired.

Veal Mexicane

Makes 4 servings

3 tablespoons flour
2 teaspoons chili powder
1 teaspoon onion salt
½ teaspoon salt
⅛ teaspoon pepper
1½ pounds veal steak, cut about ¾-inch thick
3 tablespoons fat
1 cup sour cream

1. Combine flour, chili powder, onion salt, salt, and pepper in cup.
2. Cut veal into 4 equal pieces; rub well with flour mixture.
3. Brown veal on both sides over medium heat in hot fat in Dutch oven; pour sour cream over veal; cover.
4. Simmer 20 minutes, or until meat is tender when pierced with 2-tine fork.

Veal Paprika

Makes 6 servings

2 pounds veal steak, cut ¼-inch thick
½ cup **Seasoned Flour**, page 41
3 tablespoons butter or margarine
1 clove of garlic, peeled
1½ cups water
1 cup sour cream
1½ teaspoons paprika
Buttered noodles

1. Cut veal into serving-size pieces; dust well with SEASONED FLOUR.
2. Melt butter or margarine in Dutch oven; add garlic; saute 3 minutes over low heat; remove garlic.
3. Brown meat over medium heat; add water; cover tightly.
4. Bring to boiling; reduce heat; simmer 1 hour, or until veal is tender when pierced with 2-tine fork.
5. Stir in sour cream and paprika; heat 3 minutes. (If too thick, add additional cream or milk.)
6. Serve with buttered noodles.

Veal Scallopine, Marsala

Makes 4 servings

¼ cup flour
1 teaspoon salt
¼ teaspoon pepper
⅛ teaspoon oregano
1½ pounds veal steak, cut about
     ¼-inch thick
¼ cup (½ stick) butter or margarine
¼ cup Marsala wine
1¼ cups water
2 pimientos, drained and chopped

1. Combine flour, salt, pepper, and oregano in small bowl. Cut veal into serving-size pieces about 2 inches square; dust well with flour-oregano mixture. (Use all of mixture.)
2. Melt butter or margarine in large heavy frying pan with tight-fitting cover; brown veal over medium heat 15 minutes; cover tightly.
3. Cook over low heat 15 minutes, or until meat is tender when pierced with 2-tine fork.
4. Place meat on heated platter or in chafing dish; keep hot.
5. MAKE SAUCE: Pour wine and water into frying pan; heat, stirring constantly, 5 minutes over low heat; add pimientos; simmer until sauce is hot; pour over meat.

Veal Birds

Makes 4 servings

1¼ pounds veal steak, cut about
     ¼-inch thick
1 cup (about 2 slices) soft bread crumbs
¾ teaspoon poultry seasoning
½ teaspoon salt
1 slice bacon, finely diced
1 tablespoon minced onion
1 egg, slightly beaten
2½ tablespoons **Seasoned Flour,**
     page 41
3 tablespoons butter or margarine
½ cup water

1. Cut steak into 8 strips, each about 2 by 4 inches, trimming off uneven edges; save strips for Step 3.
2. MAKE STUFFING: Grind meat trimmings in food chopper, using perforated coarse plate; combine with bread crumbs, poultry seasoning, salt, bacon, onion, and egg in medium-size bowl; toss lightly with 2-tine fork.
3. Divide stuffing into 8 equal portions; spread 1 portion over each strip of meat to within ¼-inch of edge; roll up; fasten each with small skewers or wooden picks; roll in SEASONED FLOUR.
4. Melt butter or margarine in Dutch oven; brown birds on all sides over medium heat; add water; cover tightly.
5. Bring to boiling; reduce heat; simmer 45 to 60 minutes, or until tender when pierced with 2-tine fork. Turn birds occasionally. (Add water during cooking, if needed.)
6. Place birds on platter; keep hot.
7. Make gravy following directions, page 133, using cream instead of water.

Plain Fried Veal Chops

Makes 4 servings

4 rib or loin veal chops, cut ¾-inch thick
½ teaspoon salt
⅛ teaspoon pepper
Dash of garlic salt
1 tablespoon fat

1. Sprinkle chops with salt, pepper, and garlic salt.
2. Brown on both sides over medium heat in hot fat in large heavy frying pan with tight-fitting cover; cover.
3. Simmer 20 to 25 minutes, or until tender when pierced with 2-tine fork; remove from pan; keep hot.
4. Make gravy in same pan following directions, page 133. Use half water and half milk for liquid.
5. Return chops to pan; cover tightly; heat 5 minutes.
6. Serve on heated platter; garnish with lemon slices or parsley, if desired.

Left—VEAL SCALLOPINE, MARSALA

Braised Veal Chops

Makes 4 servings

2 tablespoons flour
½ teaspoon salt
⅛ teaspoon pepper
⅛ teaspoon marjoram
⅛ teaspoon thyme
4 rib or loin veal chops,
  cut ¾-inch thick
2 tablespoons fat
1 cup water

Loin chop   *Kidney chop*

1. Combine flour, salt, pepper, marjoram, and thyme in cup; rub chops well with mixture.
2. Brown on both sides over medium heat in hot fat in large heavy frying pan with tight-fitting cover; add water; cover tightly.
3. Bring to boiling; reduce heat; simmer 45 minutes, or until tender when pierced with 2-tine fork.
4. Serve with pan gravy.

Veal Chops in Sherry Wine

Bake at 350°F about 1½ hours . . .
Makes 4 servings

3 tablespoons **Seasoned Flour,**
  page 41
½ teaspoon ground ginger
⅛ teaspoon rosemary
4 veal chops with kidneys, cut about
  1-inch thick
2 tablespoons butter or margarine
¾ cup raw rice
1 large onion, finely chopped (1 cup)
1 can (3 or 4 ounces) sliced mushrooms
1 cup dry sherry wine
1 teaspoon salt
1 cup water

1. Combine SEASONED FLOUR, ginger, and rosemary in cup; rub chops well with mixture.
2. Melt butter or margarine in large heavy frying pan; brown chops over medium heat.

3. Place rice in bottom of greased 2-quart casserole; place browned chops on rice.
4. Saute onion in same frying pan over low heat 10 to 15 minutes, or just until tender; stir in mushrooms, wine, salt, and ½ cup water; pour over veal and rice in casserole; cover tightly.
5. Bake in moderate oven (350°F) 1 hour; add remaining ½ cup water; bake ½ hour, or until veal is tender when pierced with 2-tine fork and rice is cooked through.

Braised Veal Chops, Spanish Style

Makes 4 servings

2 tablespoons **Seasoned Flour,**
  page 41
⅛ teaspoon marjoram
4 rib or loin veal chops, cut ¾-inch thick
3 tablespoons fat
1 large onion, sliced
2 cups (about 1-pound can) tomatoes
½ cup diced celery
1½ teaspoons salt
1 teaspoon sugar
¼ teaspoon pepper

1. Combine SEASONED FLOUR and marjoram in cup; rub chops well with mixture.
2. Brown on both sides over medium heat in hot fat in large heavy frying pan with tight-fitting cover; remove from pan.
3. Saute onion in same fat over low heat 10 to 15 minutes, or just until

tender; stir in tomatoes, celery, and seasonings; return chops to pan; cover tightly.

4. Simmer 50 minutes, or until meat is tender when pierced with 2-tine fork.

5. Place chops on heated platter; keep hot.

6. Make gravy following directions, page 133.

Ground Veal

To Buy *Veal patties,* made by wrapping slices of bacon around patties of ground veal, are sold in your grocery market or can be made at home. They should be braised. Veal trimmings, neck, and shank are usually ground for patties and loaves. *Mock chicken legs* are made by molding ground veal around a wooden skewer in the shape of a chicken leg. *Mock chicken* should be braised. Buy ¼ pound ground, or 1 chicken leg per serving.

To Store Wrap loosely in waxed paper or aluminum foil; store in refrigerator; use within 2 days. If frozen, store in freezer or frozen-food compartment of your refrigerator. Thaw in refrigerator or at room temperature.

Veal Loaf

Bake at 325°F about 1½ hours . . .
Makes 8 servings

1½ pounds ground veal
½ pound pork sausage meat
½ cup wheat germ
  Or: ½ cup (about 1 slice) soft bread crumbs
1 medium-size onion, finely chopped (½ cup)
1 teaspoon salt
1 teaspoon paprika
½ teaspoon celery salt
⅛ teaspoon pepper
1 egg, slightly beaten
¼ cup cream

1. Combine all ingredients in large bowl; toss together lightly with 2-tine fork. (Do not overmix.)

2. Pack into ungreased loaf pan, 9x5x3.

3. Bake in slow oven (325°F) 1½ hours, or until loaf is cooked through.

4. Serve on heated platter; garnish with sliced stuffed olives, if desired.

Taos Veal

Makes 4 servings

1 pound ground veal
¼ cup soft bread crumbs
½ teaspoon salt (for meat)
½ teaspoon rosemary
⅛ teaspoon pepper
⅛ teaspoon thyme
2 tablespoons melted butter or margarine
1 egg, slightly beaten
2 tablespoons flour
2 tablespoons fat
4 medium-size onions, sliced
½ cup diced celery
2 cups (about 1-pound can) tomatoes
1 teaspoon sugar
1 teaspoon salt (for gravy)
  Few drops bottled hot-pepper sauce
8 small potatoes, peeled

1. Combine veal, bread crumbs, salt (for meat), rosemary, pepper, thyme, melted butter or margarine, and egg in large bowl; toss together lightly with 2-tine fork. (Do not overmix.)

2. Shape into 8 balls; roll in flour.

3. Brown over medium meat in hot fat in Dutch oven; add onions and celery; saute over low heat 10 to 15 minutes, or just until onions are tender.

4. Stir in tomatoes, sugar, salt (for gravy), hot-pepper sauce, and potatoes; cover tightly.

5. Simmer 30 to 40 minutes, or until meat balls are cooked through and potatoes are tender.

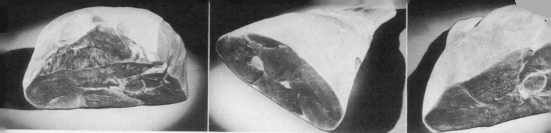

Round roast   Leg, shank half   Standing rump roast

Veal Patties

Makes 4 servings

- 1 pound ground veal
- ¾ cup (about 1½ slices) soft bread crumbs
- 2 tablespoons grated onion
- ½ teaspoon grated lemon rind
- 1 teaspoon salt
- ⅛ teaspoon pepper
- 1 egg, slightly beaten
- 2 tablespoons cream
- 4 slices bacon
- 1 tablespoon fat

1. Combine all ingredients, except bacon and fat, in large bowl; toss together with 2-tine fork. (Do not overmix.)
2. Shape into 4 patties; wrap each patty with bacon slice; fasten with skewer or wooden pick.
3. Brown on both sides over medium heat in hot fat in medium-size frying pan with tight-fitting cover; cover.
4. Cook over low heat 20 to 25 minutes, or until patties are tender and well-browned, turning once during cooking.
5. Serve on heated platter with MADEIRA-MUSHROOM SAUCE, page 129, if desired.

Veal Roasts

To Buy   *Leg* (especially the round cut from center of leg), *rib*, and *loin* of the top veal grades make the best roasts. *Sirloin, rump, leg* (of lower grades), *shoulder* and *neck* (boned and rolled), and *heel of round* are excellent for pot roasts. Buy a minimum of 3 to 4 pounds for a roast. Buy ⅓ to ½ pound, bone-in, or ¼ to ⅓ pound, boned, per serving.

To Store   Wrap loosely in waxed paper or aluminum foil; store in refrigerator; use within 1 week.

To Cook   If your roast lacks fat and has not been larded, cover with a layer

TIMETABLE
Veal†
Roasted at 325° F

Cut	Approx. Weight (lbs.)	Approx. Time (hours)	Meat Thermometer
Leg	3-8	2-4	180° F
Loin	5-6	3⅓-4	180° F
Shoulder	3-5	2-3	180° F
Rump	4-8	2⅔-4	180° F

†Time is for chilled meat from the refrigerator.

Rib roast   Loin roast   Sirloin roast

Blade roast   Arm roast   Heel of round

of suet or strips of bacon. Roast, following TIMETABLE, page 58. Let roast stand 15 minutes before carving.

Roast Veal

Roast at 325°F about 2 hours ...

4 pounds veal leg, loin, sirloin, or ribs
1 teaspoon salt
¼ teaspoon pepper
4 slices bacon, cut in halves crosswise

1. Sprinkle meat with salt and pepper; cover top with bacon slices; secure bacon with wooden picks or small skewers; place on rack, fat side up, in open roasting pan; insert meat thermometer so bulb reaches center of cut.
2. Do not add water. Do not cover.
3. Roast in slow oven (325°F) 2 hours (meat thermometer should register 180°F), or until meat is brown and tender when pierced with 2-tine fork.
4. Place meat on platter; keep hot.
5. Make gravy following directions, page 133.

Roast Stuffed Shoulder of Veal

Roast at 325°F about 2 hours ...

4 pounds veal shoulder, boned and
   pocketed for stuffing
Oyster Stuffing, page 141, or
Apricot-Walnut Stuffing, page 141
1 teaspoon salt
¼ teaspoon pepper

1. Fill pocket in meat with OYSTER STUFFING or APRICOT-WALNUT STUFFING;

fasten with skewers; tie meat with string, once lengthwise and 3 or 4 times crosswise; sprinkle with salt and pepper; place on rack, fat side up, in open roasting pan; insert meat thermometer so bulb reaches center of cut.
2. Do not add water. Do not cover.
3. Roast in slow oven (325°F) 2 hours (meat thermometer should register 180°F), or until meat is brown and tender when pierced with 2-tine fork.
4. Place meat on platter; keep hot.
5. Make gravy following directions, page 133.

Pot Roast of Veal

4 pounds veal rump, shoulder, or round,
   boned and rolled
1 tablespoon fat
½ cup water
1 tablespoon salt
½ teaspoon sugar
¼ teaspoon pepper
2 cups (about 1-pound can) tomatoes

1. Brown meat on all sides over medium heat in hot fat in Dutch oven; pour off any excess fat.
2. Add water, salt, sugar, and pepper; cover tightly.
3. Bring to boiling; reduce heat; simmer 2 hours, or until meat is tender when pierced with 2-tine fork.
4. Add tomatoes; continue cooking until tomatoes are hot.
5. Place meat on platter; keep hot.
6. Make gravy following directions, page 133.

Riblets   Breast   Fore shank

Other Cuts of Veal

To Buy *Breast* of veal is sold "bone in" or boneless. Braise or stew it. Buy 1 pound for 2 servings. *Neck* of veal is usually boned and rolled. It should be braised or stewed. Buy 1 pound for 3 to 4 servings. *Heel* of veal round is boneless and inexpensive; it should be braised or stewed. Buy 1 pound for 3 to 4 servings. *Shanks* are sold "bone in" or boneless, and are generally used for stewing or to make stock. *Flanks* are only used for stewing.

Florentine Veal

Makes 4 servings

1¼ pounds veal shoulder, rump, or
    round, cut 1-inch thick
3 tablespoons butter or margarine
1 large onion, chopped (1 cup)
1 medium-size green pepper, chopped
2 cups (about 1-pound can) tomatoes
1 teaspoon salt
¼ teaspoon pepper
1 package (8 ounces) spaghetti, cooked

1. Cut veal into 1-inch cubes.
2. Melt butter or margarine in medium-size frying pan with tight-fitting cover; brown veal over medium heat; add onion and green pepper; saute over low heat 10 to 15 minutes, or just until onion is tender.
3. Stir in tomatoes, salt, and pepper; cover tightly.
4. Simmer 1 hour, or until meat is tender when pierced with 2-tine fork.

5. Make gravy following directions, page 133. Serve veal and gravy over hot spaghetti.

Veal Rissoto à la Milanese

Makes 4 to 6 servings.

2 tablespoons butter or margarine
2 pounds veal breast, cut into bite-size
    pieces
1 medium-size onion, chopped (½ cup)
½ cup diced celery
2 tablespoons tomato paste
1 teaspoon salt
½ teaspoon sugar
¼ teaspoon pepper
2 cups boiling water
1 cup raw brown rice
¼ cup grated Parmesan cheese

1. Melt butter or margarine in Dutch oven; brown meat over medium heat; add onion and celery; saute over low heat 10 to 15 minutes, or just until onion is tender.
2. Stir in tomato paste, salt, sugar, pepper, and boiling water; cover.
3. Bring to boiling; reduce heat; simmer 1 hour; remove meat from liquid; keep hot.
4. Measure liquid; add water, if needed, to make 3 cups; bring to boiling; add rice; cook 40 minutes, or until rice is tender and liquid has been absorbed.
5. Add meat and cheese to rice mixture; reduce heat; simmer 5 minutes to heat through.

Veal and Kidney Casserole

Makes 4 servings

1 veal kidney (about ½ pound)
¼ cup **Seasoned Flour**, page 41
¼ cup (½ stick) butter or margarine
1¼ pounds veal shoulder, rump, or round,
    cut 1-inch thick
1 large onion, sliced
3 carrots, scraped and sliced
1 can (3 or 4 ounces) sliced mushrooms
½ cup water
⅓ cup dry sherry or Marsala wine
½ teaspoon salt
½ teaspoon crushed dried mint leaves
⅛ teaspoon pepper

1. Prepare kidney following directions, page 101; cut into thin slices; dust with half the SEASONED FLOUR.
2. Melt butter or margarine in Dutch oven; saute kidney over low heat 2 to 3 minutes; remove; save for Step 6.
3. Cut veal into 1-inch cubes; dust with remaining SEASONED FLOUR; brown in same pan over medium heat; add onion, carrots, and mushrooms.
4. Stir in water, wine, salt, mint, and pepper; cover tightly.
5. Bring to boiling; reduce heat; simmer 40 minutes, or until meat is tender when pierced with 2-tine fork.
6. Stir in kidney; simmer 5 minutes, or until kidney is heated through.

Veal-Onion Stew with Potato Dumplings

Makes 4 servings

1¼ pounds veal shoulder, neck, or
    shank, cut into 1-inch cubes
2½ tablespoons **Seasoned Flour**,
    page 41
2 tablespoons fat
8 medium-size onions, sliced
1 cup water
4 carrots, scraped and sliced
    Potato Dumplings, page 134

1. Dust meat well with SEASONED FLOUR.
2. Brown over medium heat in hot fat in Dutch oven.
3. Add onions; saute over low heat 10 to 15 minutes; add water; cover tightly.
4. Bring to boiling; reduce heat; simmer 1 hour; add carrots; simmer 20 minutes.
5. Drop dumplings onto top of stew; cook, uncovered, 10 to 12 minutes, or until meat and vegetables are tender when pierced with 2-tine fork and dumplings are cooked through.

Country-Style Veal and Noodles

Makes 6 servings

1½ pounds veal shoulder, cut into
    1-inch cubes
½ cup **Seasoned Flour**, page 41
2 tablespoons fat
3 cups water
3 medium-size onions, sliced
½ cup chopped green pepper
1 clove of garlic, minced
1 package (8 ounces) noodles, cooked
    and drained
1 cup sour cream
1 tablespoon paprika
1½ teaspoons salt
⅛ teaspoon pepper

1. Dust meat well with SEASONED FLOUR; brown over medium heat in hot fat in large heavy frying pan with tight-fitting cover.
2. Add water, onions, green pepper, and garlic; cover tightly.
3. Bring to boiling; reduce heat; simmer 1½ hours, or until veal is tender when pierced with 2-tine fork.
4. Add noodles, sour cream, paprika, salt, and pepper; simmer until mixture is piping hot.

Ways with Leftover Veal...

Veal and Rice Casserole

Bake at 350° F about 30 minutes ...
Makes 4 servings

¼ cup raw rice
1½ cups **Medium White Sauce,**
    page 128
  2 cups cubed cooked veal
¼ cup chopped stuffed olives
¼ cup diced celery
  1 teaspoon salt
⅛ teaspoon pepper

1. Cook rice in boiling, salted water in large saucepan 20 minutes (rice will be almost tender); drain thoroughly.
2. Combine rice, WHITE SAUCE, veal, olives, celery, salt, and pepper in greased 1½-quart casserole.
3. Bake in moderate oven (350° F) 30 minutes, or until heated through.

Curried Veal in Rice Ring

Bake at 350° F about 30 minutes ...
Makes 4 servings

  3 cups cooked rice
¼ cup (½ stick) melted butter
    or margarine
½ teaspoon salt
  2 tablespoons finely chopped pimiento
  2 cups cubed cooked veal
  2 cups **Curry Sauce,** page 130
    Chopped parsley

1. Combine rice, melted butter or margarine, salt, and pimiento in medium-size bowl; pack rice mixture into well-greased 1-quart ring mold.
2. Bake in moderate oven (350° F) 30 minutes, or until rice ring is firm and shrinks slightly from sides.
3. Combine veal and CURRY SAUCE in medium-size saucepan with tight-fitting cover; cover.

4. Heat through slowly.
5. Turn out rice ring onto heated platter; fill center with hot veal mixture; garnish with chopped parsley.

Veal and Mushroom Aspic

Makes 6 servings

  1 envelope unflavored gelatin
  1 can (12 ounces) mixed vegetable juice
1½ cups diced cooked veal
  1 can (3 or 4 ounces) sliced mushrooms
  2 tablespoons finely chopped parsley
  1 tablespoon finely chopped pimiento
1½ teaspoons grated onion
  1 teaspoon salt
¼ teaspoon poultry seasoning
    Tomato wedges

1. Soften gelatin in ¼ cup vegetable juice in small bowl.
2. Heat remaining 1¼ cups juice; add to gelatin mixture; stir until dissolved; chill until syrupy.
3. Combine veal, mushrooms, parsley, pimiento, onion, salt, and poultry seasoning in medium-size bowl; toss together lightly.
4. Stir syrupy gelatin into meat mixture.
5. Spoon into lightly oiled loaf pan, 9x5x3; chill until firm.
6. Unmold on platter; garnish with tomato wedges.

Veal Cakes

Makes 4 servings

  3 tablespoons butter or margarine
  2 cups coarsely ground cooked veal
  1 cup grated raw potato
  1 teaspoon salt
  1 teaspoon curry powder
  2 tablespoons fat

1. Cream butter or margarine in medium-size bowl; add veal, potato, salt, and curry powder; toss together lightly with 2-tine fork.
2. Shape into 8 half-inch-thick cakes.
3. Fry on both sides in hot fat in large heavy frying pan over medium heat 10 minutes, or until brown.
4. Place cakes on heated platter. Serve with chutney or pickle relish, if desired.

Veal and Pimiento Timbales

Bake at 325°F about 30 minutes . . . Makes 4 servings

    3 eggs, separated
    ⅓ cup cream
    1½ cups finely ground cooked veal
    2 pimientos, finely diced
    3 tablespoons dry sherry or Marsala
      wine
    ½ teaspoon salt (for meat)
    ⅛ teaspoon pepper
    ¼ teaspoon salt (for egg whites)
    Mushroom Sauce, page 131

1. Beat egg yolks in medium-size bowl; stir in cream, veal, pimientos, wine, salt (for meat), and pepper.
2. Beat egg whites with salt (for egg whites) until very stiff; fold lightly into veal mixture.
3. Spoon meat mixture into 4 well-greased, 6-ounce molds or custard cups (if your molds are smaller, fill them only ⅔ full); place in pan of hot water (water should be level with veal mixture in molds).
4. Bake in slow oven (325°F) 30 minutes, or until firmly set, or knife, inserted in center, comes out clean.
5. Cool 3 minutes; loosen around edges with small spatula or knife; unmold onto heated platter. Serve with MUSHROOM SAUCE.

Veal Menus

Crabmeat Cocktail
Veal and Mushroom Aspic*
Parsley New Potatoes
Creamed Carrots and Peas
Mixed Green Salad   French Dressing
Finger Rolls   Butter
Fruit Compote
Beverage

* *

Veal Loaf*
Buttered Lima Beans   Mashed Potatoes
Minted Pineapple Salad
Rolls   Butter
Custard Bread Pudding
Beverage

* *

Fruit Cup
Roast Veal*
Baked Potato
Broccoli with Hollandaise Sauce
Romaine Salad with Russian Dressing
Bread   Butter
Butterscotch Cream
Beverage

* *

Curried Veal in Rice Ring*
Chutney, Coconut, Chopped Nuts
Lettuce Wedges   Roquefort Dressing
Rolls   Butter
Baked Apple   Cream
Beverage

*For recipes see index

63

Lamb and Mutton

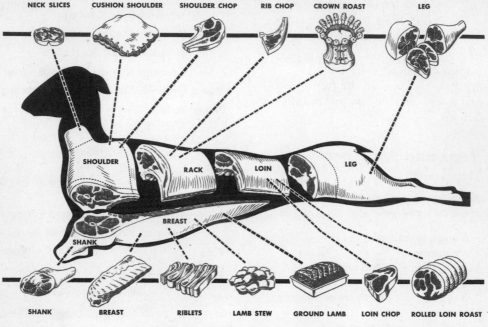

NECK SLICES CUSHION SHOULDER SHOULDER CHOP RIB CHOP CROWN ROAST LEG

SHOULDER RACK LOIN LEG

BREAST

SHANK

SHANK BREAST RIBLETS LAMB STEW GROUND LAMB LOIN CHOP ROLLED LOIN ROAST

Wholesale and retail cuts of lamb

Make lamb a favorite at your house. Each of these recipes will add delightful variety to your menus. To serve it at its best, take care in cooking lamb. Overcooking, especially, makes it leathery grayish brown and unappetizing. Cooked just to the proper degree of faintly-pink doneness, it is mild in flavor, tender, and juicy. Broiling and roasting may be used more often with lamb than with any other type of meat, since lamb usually is tender, well finished, and juicy.

When you buy "spring" lamb you are buying the meat of lambs up to 12 months old. "Genuine spring" lamb is the term used for meat from lambs less than 5 months old. "Spring" lamb is sold the year around. "Genuine spring" lamb is marketed usually just before Easter as "Easter lambs" or in early summer. "Hothouse" lamb is 5 to 8 weeks old. It comes on the market very early in the season, is expensive, very tender and delicate in flavor, but is flabby and watery in texture.

Lamb lean is pinkish to deep red in color and has a smooth covering of brittle pinkish-white fat. Mutton varies from dark pink to dark red in color. You can judge the age of the lamb you are buying by the break joint. This is the joint at which the fore feet are removed. In young lambs this is smooth, moist, and red. In the meat of older sheep (mutton) this is white. Mutton is the meat of sheep over 1 year old. Only about 10% of the sheep meat sold in the United States is mutton.

All lamb sold in interstate commerce is Government inspected and marked with the stamp "U. S. Inspected and Passed." Lamb and mutton may also be graded as U. S. Prime, U. S. Choice,

U. S. Good, U. S. Commercial, U. S. Utility, and U. S. Cull, or branded by the individual packer.

Lamb and mutton are graded on age, conformation, finish, and quality. Usually, the younger the animal, the better the grade of lamb. Lamb and mutton carcasses have good conformation when they are short and stocky in build with full thick legs, loins, ribs, and chucks. They have a high proportion of meat to bone.

Lamb should have an even covering of fat ¼ to ½ inch thick over the outside and much marbling. The lean has a velvety feel, is firm and fine textured. Poor quality is indicated by a soft, watery or gummy feel.

U. S. Choice is the highest grade generally sold. U. S. Utility and Cull are rarely sold in grocery markets.

Grade for grade, mutton sells often for less than half the price per pound of lamb. If you enjoy its flavor, it is a specially good buy.

The thin, papery covering over lamb is called the "fell." This may be left on or removed.

Lamb Steaks and Chops

To Buy *Loin chops* are cut from the part of the sheep corresponding to that of beef from which porterhouse, T-bone, and club steaks are cut. These are a luxury meat cut. When cut from Prime, Choice, or Good carcasses, they should be an inch thick and broiled.

Chops from lower grades should be fried. Buy 1 chop per serving.

English chops are double loin chops, unsplit through the back bone. When the loin or English chops contain slices of kidney, they are known as kidney chops and English kidney chops. Buy 1 double chop for a large serving.

Rib chops are smaller than loin chops. They should be cut thick and broiled. They are known as *French chops* when the meat is trimmed from the end of the bone and the bone is covered with a chop frill before serving. Buy 1 to 2 chops per serving.

Sirloin chops are cut from heavy legs. They correspond to the sirloin steaks cut from beef. Buy 1 large chop about 1″ thick for 2 servings and broil.

Shoulder chops are divided into *chuck, rib,* and *shoulder arm.* These are the most economical lamb chops and if of good grade can be broiled. Braise the lower grades. Buy 1 chop per serving.

Lamb steaks contain a small amount of bone and are economical, but are not cut in many meat markets. They are cut from large legs. Buy 1 to 1¼ pounds for 4 servings.

To Store Wrap loosely in waxed paper or aluminum foil; store flat in your refrigerator. Use within 5 days.

To Cook All lamb chops and steaks of the better grades can be broiled. Buy chops 1 to 2 inches thick for broiling. Thinner chops may be pan-broiled. Shoulder chops are often braised.

Loin chops   *Rib chops*   *English chops*

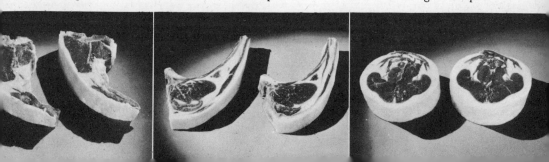

TO BROIL   Season lamb chops with salt and pepper, with garlic salt, or brush with French dressing before broiling.

TO PAN-BROIL   Rub chops with cut clove of garlic, if desired. Rub heavy frying pan with piece of fat cut from edge of chop; brown on both sides over medium heat; cook until chops are done the way you like them; season with salt and pepper or salt and garlic salt; serve piping hot on heated platter with pan gravy (see page 132), if desired.

Braised Shoulder Chops, Maryland

Makes 4 servings

4 shoulder lamb chops, cut
    about ¾ inch thick
1 small onion, finely chopped (¼ cup)
½ cup water
1 teaspoon salt
½ teaspoon crushed dried mint leaves
    Few drops bottled hot-pepper sauce
1 package quick-frozen lima beans
2 tablespoons butter or margarine
1 tablespoon chopped chives

1.   Trim small amount of fat from edges of chops; render in large heavy frying pan with tight-fitting cover; remove rendered trimmings; brown chops over medium heat; push to one side.
2.   Saute onion over low heat in same pan 5 minutes, or just until tender; stir in water, salt, mint, and hot-pepper sauce; cover tightly.

3.   Bring to boiling; reduce heat; simmer 30 minutes, or until meat is tender when pierced with 2-tine fork.
4.   Cook lima beans while meat cooks, following directions on package; season with butter or margarine and chopped chives.
5.   Place lima beans on heated platter; surround with chops; keep hot.
6.   Make gravy following directions, page 133, substituting 1 cup milk for the water.

Lorraine's Lamb Steaks

Makes 4 servings

4 lamb steaks, cut 1 inch thick
    Melted butter or margarine
    Salt and pepper
    Hot Mint Sauce, page 132

1.   Brush steaks with butter or margarine.
2.   Broil, with top of meat 3 inches from unit or tip of flame, for half the time needed using TIMETABLE, page 67; season cooked side with salt and pepper; turn steaks; finish broiling and seasoning. Serve with HOT MINT SAUCE.

Philadelphia Lamb Grill

Makes 4 servings

4 loin lamb chops, cut 1 inch thick
2 lamb kidneys, halved
    Salt and pepper
    Peppermint-Pineapple Slices,
    page 139

1.   Wrap tail of chop around lamb

Sirloin chops   *Patties*   *Shoulder chops*

kidney half; fasten with small skewer or wooden pick.

2. Broil, with top of meat 3 inches from unit or tip of flame, for half the time needed using TIMETABLE at right; season cooked side; turn chops.

3. Place unbroiled PEPPERMINT-PINEAPPLE SLICES next to chops; finish broiling and seasoning.

Ground Lamb

To Buy Trimmings, shoulder, shank, and neck can be ground for patties or lamb loaf. Choose meat that is not too fatty when having it ground to order.

Lamb patties are often made by your meatman from ground lamb, and wrapped with a strip of bacon. These weigh 4 to 6 ounces. Buy 1 per serving.

To Store Wrap loosely in waxed paper or aluminum foil; store in coldest part of refrigerator; use within 24 hours.

Lamb Loaf

Bake at 325° F about 1 hour . . .
Makes 6 to 8 servings

   1 cup (about 2 slices) soft bread crumbs
   ¼ cup milk
   2 pounds ground lamb
   1 small onion, finely chopped (¼ cup)
   1 egg, slightly beaten
   2 teaspoons salt
   ¼ teaspoon pepper

1. Soak bread crumbs in milk in large bowl until milk is absorbed.

2. Add lamb, onion, egg, salt, and pepper; toss together lightly with 2-tine fork. (Do not overmix.)

3. Pack into baking pan, 9x5x3.

4. Bake in slow oven (325°F) 1 hour, or until meat is cooked the way you like it.

5. Place loaf on platter; keep hot.

6. Make gravy following directions, page 133, or serve with FLORENTINE SAUCE, page 129, if desired.

Cut	Approx. Thickness (inches)	Approx. Time (min.)
Rib or Loin Chops	1	12-14
	1½	18-20
Double Chops	2	22-30
Shoulder Chops	1	16-18
Leg Steaks	1	16-18
Patties	1	20-22
Mutton Chops	1	20-22

†Time is for chilled meat from the refrigerator.

Lamburgers

Makes 4 servings

   1 pound ground lamb
   1 teaspoon salt
   ⅛ teaspoon pepper
   Dash of garlic powder
   Fat, butter, or margarine for frying

1. Combine lamb, salt, pepper, and garlic powder in medium-size bowl, toss together lightly with 2-tine fork. (Do not overmix.)

2. Shape into 4 patties.

3. Fry on both sides over medium heat in hot fat in medium-size frying pan 20 to 25 minutes, or until meat is cooked the way you like it.

Chop onion, parsley, garlic, or green pepper on a board using sharp French knife.

Crown roast   "American" leg   "Frenched" leg

Lamb and Mutton Roasts

To Buy Leg, shoulder, rib, and loin cuts are sold for roasts.

The *leg* is sold as a full leg weighing 5 to 9 pounds either "American" or "French" style. For American style the long leg bone at the small end of the cut is removed and the meat is tucked into the thick part of the leg. This makes the roast more compact. For a French leg, the bone is left in and covered with a paper frill just before serving. Or the leg is cut into a *sirloin* and a *round* roast. A sirloin roast is difficult to carve unless it is boned and rolled. It is usually the smallest lamb roast, weighing 2 to 3 pounds, and is especially nice for small families. The *round* roast is very desirable because it

is easy to carve and makes a wonderful company roast. Boned and rolled, half or whole legs are also sold.

Three styles of roast are made from the shoulder: square-cut with the bones in, cushion (a boned, square-cut), and boned and rolled. These are cheaper than the leg, are smaller, generally, and are very versatile. The shoulder is used not only for roasts and pot roasts, but is also ground for patties or loaf, or cut up for stew or for broiling (shish kebab).

The ribs and loins from large carcasses are cut as roasts. These are expensive.

One of the most attractive roasts you can buy, however, is made from the rib cut—a crown roast of lamb. This is easily carved but very very expensive—

TIMETABLE
Lamb†
Roasted at 325°F

Cut	Approx. Weight (lbs.)	Approx. Time (hours)	Meat Thermometer
Leg (full)	8-9	4-4½	175°F (med.)
		4½-5	182°F (well)
Leg ("American")	5-6	2½-3	175°F (med.)
		3-3½	182°F (well)
Crown	5-6	3½-4½	182°F
Shoulder	3-5	1¾-3	182°F
Rolled Shoulder	3-4	2-2½	182°F

†Time is for chilled meat from the refrigerator.

Loin roast   *Boneless sirloin roast*   *Cushion shoulder*

a wonderful roast for a very special occasion. It is only cut to order. To make it, two rib portions are sewed or tied together to form a circle or crown. Mutton roasts of similar cut and grade can be cooked just as lamb is cooked.

To Store Wrap meat loosely in waxed paper or aluminum foil. Store in your refrigerator. Use within 5 days. If meat is frozen, store in your freezer or frozen-food compartment of your refrigerator. Thaw in refrigerator or roast unthawed.

Crown Roast of Lamb

Roast at 325° F about 3 hours . . .

> 1 crown roast of lamb*
> Bacon
> Salt and pepper

1. Wrap chop bones with bacon (or use aluminum foil) to prevent charring; season roast with salt and pepper.
2. Place crown upright on rack in open roasting pan; insert meat thermometer so bulb reaches center of cut. (If you have no thermometer, weigh roast, then figure time needed using TIMETABLE, page 68.)
3. Do not add water. Do not cover pan.

*Small crown of lamb contains about 10 chops and weighs 3 to 4 pounds after trimming; a large crown contains 16 or more chops. Allow 2 chops per serving. The center of the crown may be filled with ground lamb trimmings or with stuffing, if desired. If center is filled, roasting time will be increased, since this makes roast more compact. Have meatman prepare roast. Backbone must be cut off to make carving easy.

4. Roast in slow oven (325° F), depending on its weight for time needed (roast is compact and needs long cooking), or until thermometer registers 182° F.
5. Place meat on heated platter; remove coverings from bones; decorate with chop frills; keep hot.
6. Make gravy following directions, page 133.
7. Serve roast surrounded by new potatoes and peas or carrots, if desired.

Roast Leg of Lamb

Roast at 325° F about 3 hours . . .

> 1 leg of lamb (5 to 6 pounds)
> 1 clove of garlic, cut
> ¼ cup **Seasoned Flour**, page 41
> **Mint Sauce**, page 132

1. Rub meat well with garlic and SEASONED FLOUR. (Do not remove the fell or thin papery covering, since this helps keep meat juicy.)
2. Place on rack, fat side up, in open roasting pan; insert meat thermometer so bulb reaches center of cut. (If you have no thermometer, weigh roast, then figure time needed using TIMETABLE, page 68.)
3. Do not add water. Do not cover.
4. Roast in slow oven (325° F) for the time needed, or until thermometer registers 175° F (medium) or 182° F (well done).
5. Place meat on platter; keep hot.
6. Make gravy following directions, page 133.

Above—LAMBURGERS, *page 67, with dilled new potatoes and green peas*

VARIATIONS

Roast Shoulder of Lamb Prepare a rolled shoulder weighing 3½ to 5 pounds following directions for roast leg, page 69. Roast according to TIME-TABLE, page 68.

Roast Stuffed Shoulder of Lamb Stuff a *cushion shoulder* of lamb weighing 3 to 4 pounds with BREAD AND BUT-TER STUFFING, page 140. Roast following directions, page 69 and according to TIMETABLE, page 68.

Braised Mutton

1 small leg of mutton (about 7 pounds)
2 medium-size onions, sliced
    Bouquet garni (see inside back cover)
6 peppercorns
2 cloves of garlic, quartered
1 tablespoon salt
⅛ teaspoon pepper

1. Place mutton in very large heavy kettle with tight-fitting cover or Dutch oven; add remaining ingredients; half

cover meat with boiling water; cove. tightly.

2. Simmer 2 to 2½ hours, or until tender when pierced with 2-tine fork.

3. Place meat on heated platter; keep hot.

4. Make gravy following directions, page 133.

5. Serve with currant jelly or HOT MINT SAUCE, page 132, if desired.

Lamb Pot Roast

4 pounds lamb shoulder, boned and rolled
1 teaspoon salt
½ teaspoon oregano
¼ teaspoon pepper
1½ cups boiling water
1 cup diced celery
1 cup fresh lima beans
6 carrots, scraped and quartered
12 small white onions, peeled (about ½ pound)

1. Brown fatty side of lamb, then remaining sides over medium heat in large heavy kettle with tight-fitting cover, or Dutch oven.

2. Sprinkle lamb with salt, oregano and pepper; add boiling water; cover tightly.

3. Simmer about 1½ hours, or until meat is almost tender.

4. Add celery, lima beans, carrots, and onions; simmer 30 minutes, or until meat and vegetables are tender when pierced with 2-tine fork.

5. Place meat on heated platter; keep hot.

6. Strain vegetables from drippings; save for Step 8.

7. Make gravy following directions, page 133.

8. Reheat vegetables in gravy; serve with lamb.

Other Cuts of Lamb

Neck, shank, and *breast* are the least expensive cuts of lamb. These are usually braised or stewed (shoulder and leg are also sometimes braised or stewed). Buy 1 pound neck for 4 servings or 1 shank per serving. Lamb *breasts* are sometimes pocketed for stuffing, boned, and rolled for pot roasting, or cut into riblets to be cooked in a sauce. Breasts are 1 to 2 inches thick, weigh about 2 pounds, and are fatty. Buy 2 pounds for 4 servings.

Curried Lamb

Makes 6 servings

1½ pounds boned shoulder or shank of lamb, cut into 1-inch cubes
1½ tablespoons flour
1 tablespoon curry powder
1 teaspoon salt
½ teaspoon celery salt
¼ teaspoon garlic salt
1 large onion, sliced
½ cup water
2 medium-size tart apples, pared, cored, and diced
1 tablespoon sugar

1. Trim small amount of fat from meat; render over low heat in large heavy frying pan with tight-fitting cover; remove rendered trimmings.

2. Combine flour, curry powder, salt, celery salt, and garlic salt in paper bag; dust meat in mixture.

3. Saute onion in hot fat over low heat 10 to 15 minutes, or just until tender; push aside in pan; brown meat over medium heat.

4. Stir in water, apples, remaining flour mixture, and sugar; cover tightly.

5. Bring to boiling; reduce heat; simmer 1½ hours, or until meat is tender when pierced with 2-tine fork.

6. Serve with cooked rice, if desired.

Armenian Lamb

Makes 4 servings

2 pounds shoulder of lamb, cut into
    1-inch cubes
¼ cup flour
2 teaspoons salt
1 teaspoon crushed dried mint leaves
½ teaspoon mace
⅛ teaspoon garlic salt
⅛ teaspoon pepper
1 pound mushrooms, sliced
½ cup tomato juice

1. Trim small amount of fat from meat; render over low heat in large heavy frying pan with tight-fitting cover; remove rendered trimmings.
2. Combine flour, salt, mint, mace, garlic salt, and pepper in pie plate; roll meat in flour mixture.
3. Brown meat over medium heat in hot fat; stir in mushrooms and tomato juice; cover tightly.
4. Bring to boiling; reduce heat; simmer 45 minutes, or until meat is tender when pierced with 2-tine fork. Serve with fluffy rice, if desired.

Barbecued Lamb Shanks

Makes 4 servings

4 lamb shanks (about 2 pounds)
¼ cup **Seasoned Flour**, page 41
2 tablespoons fat
½ cup catsup
½ cup water
1 tablespoon brown sugar
2 tablespoons Worcestershire sauce
2 tablespoons vinegar
1 tablespoon lemon juice
½ teaspoon MSG (monosodium
    glutamate)

1. Rub meat well with SEASONED FLOUR; brown on all sides over medium heat in hot fat in large heavy frying pan with tight-fitting cover; pour off any excess fat.

2. Combine remaining ingredients in small bowl; pour over meat; cover.
3. Bring to boiling; reduce heat; simmer 1 hour, or until meat is tender when pierced with 2-tine fork.
4. Place meat on heated platter; spoon sauce over meat.

Mutton Stew

Makes 4 servings

2 pounds shank or neck of mutton, cut
    into bite-size pieces
2 large onions, sliced
2 teaspoons salt
1½ teaspoons crushed dried mint leaves
1 teaspoon celery salt
¼ teaspoon pepper
1 bay leaf
2 cups boiling water
4 carrots, scraped and quartered
1 package quick-frozen peas
Curried Dumplings, page 134

1. Combine meat, onions, salt, mint, celery salt, pepper, bay leaf, and boiling water in large heavy saucepan with tight-fitting cover; cover tightly.
2. Simmer 1¼ hours, or until meat is almost tender when pierced with fork.
3. Add carrots and peas; cook 15 minutes, or until vegetables are tender.
4. MAKE DUMPLINGS: Prepare ½ recipe for CURRIED DUMPLINGS; cook, following directions for dumplings.

Lamb Riblets, Monterrey

Makes 4 servings

1 large onion, chopped (1 cup)
1 tablespoon olive oil
2 pounds lamb riblets
1 clove of garlic, sliced
3 tablespoons vinegar
3 tablespoons lemon juice
2 tablespoons brown sugar
¾ cup catsup
½ cup water
1 teaspoon salt
⅛ teaspoon pepper

Neck slices   *Riblets*   *Shanks*

1. Saute onion in hot olive oil in large heavy frying pan with tight-fitting cover over low heat 10 to 15 minutes, or just until tender; push to one side; brown meat on all sides in same pan over medium heat.

2. Add remaining ingredients; cover tightly.

3. Bring to boiling; reduce heat; simmer 1 hour, or until meat is tender when pierced with 2-tine fork.

4. Place riblets on heated platter; spoon sauce over meat. (This is a treat for anyone who loves fatty meats.)

Merry-Go-Around Lamb

Makes 8 generous servings of stew or 8 individual pies
Bake at 425°F for 25 to 30 minutes

> 2 pounds lamb neck, shoulder, breast, or shank, cut into 1-inch cubes
> ½ cup **Seasoned Flour**, page 41
> 2 tablespoons fat
> 1 clove of garlic
> 1 medium-size onion, sliced
> 1 bay leaf
> 8 carrots, scraped and quartered
> 24 small white onions, peeled (about 1 pound)
> 6 potatoes, pared and quartered
> 1 cup diced celery
> 1 teaspoon salt
> ½ teaspoon marjoram
> 1 cup cooked or canned peas
> 2 packages piecrust mix (for pies)

1. Dust meat well with SEASONED FLOUR placed in paper bag.

2. Heat fat with garlic in 4-quart saucepan with tight-fitting cover or Dutch oven; brown meat, a few pieces at a time, in hot fat over medium heat.

3. Pour off any excess fat; return all browned meat to pan; add enough boiling water just to cover meat; add sliced onion and bay leaf; cover tightly.

4. Bring to boiling; reduce heat; simmer, stirring occasionally, 1½ hours.

5. Add carrots, onions, potatoes, celery, salt, and marjoram; simmer 25 minutes, or until meat and vegetables are tender when pierced with fork.

6. Make gravy following directions, page 133.

7. Add peas; heat through. Serve immediately as stew.

8. TO MAKE INDIVIDUAL PIES: Fill 8 12-ounce casseroles with stew. Prepare pastry according to directions on package of mix; roll out half of dough ⅛-inch thick on lightly floured pastry cloth or board; mark 8 pastry circles ½-inch larger in diameter than the casseroles; cut out center of each round with star-shaped cooky cutter. Place 1 pastry circle on each casserole; press dough to edge of casserole.

9. Roll remaining pastry to long rectangle (length should be twice the circumference of casserole) ⅛ inch thick; cut into ½-inch-wide strips; holding 2 strips between thumb and index finger in one hand, gently roll and twist them together with other hand. Moisten pastry edge; place rolled strips on moistened area; secure with fingertips. See photograph on back of book.

10. Bake in hot oven (425°F) 25 to 30 minutes, or until crust is lightly browned.

Ways with Leftover Lamb...

Baked Lamb Hash

Bake at 350°F about 25 minutes...
Makes 4 servings

2 cups ground cooked lamb
1 can (3 or 4 ounces) chopped
  mushrooms
1 cup (about 2 slices) soft bread crumbs
1 medium-size onion, finely chopped
  (½ cup)
1 pimiento, chopped
1 egg, slightly beaten
1 teaspoon salt
¼ teaspoon pepper
¼ teaspoon thyme
Thick White Sauce, page 128

1. Combine all ingredients in medium-size bowl; toss together lightly with 2-tine fork.
2. Spoon mixture into 4 six-ounce custard cups.
3. Bake in moderate oven (350°F) 25 minutes, or until slightly browned.
4. Unmold onto heated platter. Serve with chili sauce, if desired.

Lamb à la King in Casserole

Bake at 375°F about 30 minutes...
Makes 4 servings

5 cups hot seasoned mashed potatoes
  (about 6 medium-size)
¼ cup (½ stick) butter or margarine
¼ cup flour
1 teaspoon salt
2 cups milk
2 cups cooked lamb, cut into ½-inch
  cubes
1 cup drained cooked or canned peas
1 small onion, grated
2 pimientos, diced

1. Spread mashed potatoes in even layer over bottom and around sides of buttered 1½-quart baking dish.

2. Melt butter or margarine in medium-size saucepan; blend in flour and salt; slowly stir in milk; cook over low heat, stirring constantly, until mixture thickens and boils 1 minute.
3. Stir in lamb, peas, onion, and pimientos; pour mixture into potato-lined baking dish.
4. Bake in moderate oven (375°F) 30 minutes, or until potato border is lightly browned.

Stuffed Eggplant

Bake at 350°F about 1 hour, 20 minutes
Makes 4 servings

2 small eggplants
1 cup boiling water
1 medium-size onion, finely chopped
  (½ cup)
2 tablespoons fat
2 cups ground cooked lamb
1 raw carrot, finely diced
1 tablespoon chopped chives
½ teaspoon salt
⅛ teaspoon pepper
⅛ teaspoon cinnamon
  Florentine Sauce, page 129
  (omit wine)

1. Cut eggplants in half lengthwise; place, cut side down, in large shallow baking pan containing ¼-inch depth of water.
2. Bake in moderate oven (350°F) 1 hour, or until tender when pierced with 2-tine fork.
3. MAKE STUFFING: While eggplants bake, saute onion in hot fat in medium-size frying pan with tight-fitting cover over low heat 5 minutes, or just until tender; stir in lamb, carrot, chives, salt, pepper, and cinnamon; cover tightly.
4. Simmer 5 minutes.
5. Remove eggplant halves from baking pan; pour off any remaining water; return halves to pan, cut sides up.

6. Spread stuffing over tops of halves; pour hot FLORENTINE SAUCE over each half.

7. Bake in moderate oven (350° F) 20 to 25 minutes, or until heated through.

VARIATION

German Stuffed Eggplant Substitute 2 cups (about ½ pound) ground knockwurst for the lamb in Step 3.

Baked Lamb and Rice

Bake at 350° F about 50 minutes . . . Makes 4 servings

> 2 tablespoons butter or margarine
> 1 medium-size onion, finely chopped (½ cup)
> **Or:** 1 bunch green onions, trimmed and chopped
> 1 teaspoon celery salt
> 1 teaspoon Worcestershire sauce
> ½ teaspoon salt
> ⅛ teaspoon pepper
> 1¼ cups chopped cooked lamb
> 1 cup cooked rice (about ¼ cup raw)
> ¼ cup India relish
> 1 egg, well beaten
> ⅔ cup milk

1. Melt butter or margarine in large heavy frying pan; saute onion over low heat 5 minutes, or just until tender.

2. Stir in celery salt, Worcestershire sauce, salt, pepper, lamb, rice, and India relish.

3. Combine egg and milk; add to meat mixture.

4. Pack into greased 1-quart casserole; place in pan of hot water (water should be 1 inch deep).

5. Bake in moderate oven (350° F) 50 minutes, or until piping hot and slightly browned.

6. Serve with hot leftover lamb gravy or HOT MINT SAUCE, page 132, if desired.

Lamb Menus

Merry-Go-Around Lamb*
Perfection Salad
Hot Corn Muffins   Butter
Gingerbread with Hard Sauce
Beverage

* *

Cream of Celery Soup   Crackers
Armenian Lamb*
Rice   Spinach
Carrot and Pineapple Salad
Minted Grapefruit
Beverage

* *

Orange Compote
Stuffed Eggplant*
Green Beans
Hot Biscuits   Butter
Ice Cream
Beverage

* *

Jellied Consomme
Roast Leg of Lamb*
Hot Mint Sauce*
Whipped Potatoes   New Peas
Bread   Butter
Strawberry Shortcake
Beverage

* *

Broiled Lamb Chops*
Creamed Potatoes   New Peas
Hot Rolls   Butter
Pineapple Cream-Cheese Salad
Chocolate Souffle
Beverage

For recipes see index

Pork

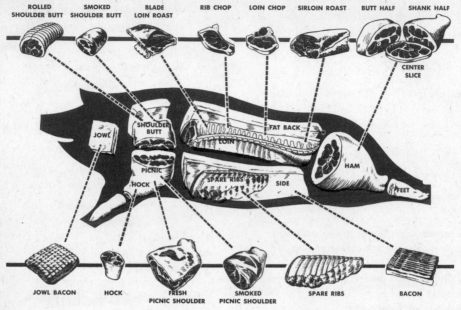

ROLLED SHOULDER BUTT SMOKED SHOULDER BUTT BLADE LOIN ROAST RIB CHOP LOIN CHOP SIRLOIN ROAST BUTT HALF SHANK HALF

CENTER SLICE

JOWL SHOULDER BUTT FAT BACK LOIN HAM

PICNIC SPARE RIBS SIDE FEET

HOCK

JOWL BACON HOCK FRESH PICNIC SHOULDER SMOKED PICNIC SHOULDER SPARE RIBS BACON

Wholesale and retail cuts of pork

Pork is the rich-flavored, well marbled meat of hogs. Its distinctive flavor is due to the fat. Good quality pork comes from animals 7 to 12 months old. Pork does not vary as much in tenderness and flavor as do other meats because hogs are bred solely for meat and are marketed young and well finished. Even brood sows usually are marketed before they are three years old.

Grading for quality has been done by individual packers under brand names, but until 1952 the U. S. Government did not grade pork. The U. S. Grades now established are U. S. Choice, U. S. Medium, and U. S. Cull. These are based upon the yields of lean and fat cuts and upon the quality of the meat. U. S. Choice carcasses yield the largest percentage of lean cuts. Grade identification does not appear on retail cuts of pork.

All pork moving in interstate commerce is Federally inspected and stamped as a guarantee of its wholesomeness. The presence of *trichinae* (pork parasites) however, may escape notice. For this reason *fresh pork must be thoroughly cooked before eating* (no pink color should remain).

Pork is sold fresh and cured. Fresh pork is most plentiful between November and March and accounts for a little more than one third of the total amount of pork used. Cured pork, such as bacon, ham, picnic, shoulder butt, and salt pork account for the remaining sales.

Quality pork has a grayish-pink, fine-textured, firm lean, and firm white fat on the outside with some marbling. The bones are reddish. Heavy marbling or fat layers in the lean are signs of poor quality.

Fresh pork (for cured pork, see page 85) is roasted, simmered, or braised. Broiling is not recommended.

Pork cuts are fewer in number and

| Arm steak | Blade steak | Loin chops |

do not closely resemble those of beef. The loin and rib sections are cut as one, and the round and rump are cut as whole ham. For other variations, compare the charts pages 14 and 76.

Pork cuts are often divided into lean (loin, picnic, ham, Boston butt, Canadian bacon, and spareribs) and fat (jowl, belly, brisket, fat back, and clear plate). Pork cuts vary in different sections of the United States.

Pork Steaks and Chops

To Buy Chops cut from the *loin* are "center cut" or "end." Center cut is preferred. *Shoulder* chops include *blade-bone* (much bone) and *round-bone* chops (small bone). Rib and center-cut chops are generally cut 1 inch thick, shoulder-end loin chops about ½ inch thick, and shoulder chops ⅓ to ½ inch thick. Buy 1 to 2 chops per serving.
Pork steaks are cut from the ham and have only a small round bone. Pork cutlets are boned steaks.
To Store Wrap loosely in waxed paper or aluminum foil; store flat in your refrigerator. Use within 3 days.

Barbecued Pork Shoulder Steaks

Makes 4 servings

    4 pork shoulder steaks, cut ½ inch thick
    2 tablespoons fat
      Hot Barbecue Sauce, page 131

1. Brown steaks well on both sides over medium heat in hot fat in large heavy frying pan with tight-fitting cover.
2. Pour HOT BARBECUE SAUCE over chops in pan; cover tightly.
3. Simmer 45 minutes, or until tender when pierced with 2-tine fork. (Add water during cooking to prevent sticking, if needed.)
4. Place chops on heated platter; spoon sauce over meat.

Pork Shoulder Steaks, Pierre

Makes 4 servings

    3 tablespoons flour
    ¼ teaspoon salt
    ⅛ teaspoon thyme
    4 pork shoulder steaks, cut ½ inch thick
    2 tablespoons fat
   16 dried apricot halves
    4 teaspoons brown sugar
    ¼ teaspoon ground ginger
    1 cup hot water

1. Combine flour, salt, and thyme in cup; rub steaks with mixture.
2. Brown steaks well on both sides over medium heat in hot fat in large heavy frying pan with tight-fitting cover.
3. Place 4 apricot halves, cut side down, on each steak; combine brown sugar and ginger in cup; sprinkle apricots with mixture; add water; cover tightly.
4. Simmer 45 minutes, or until meat is tender when pierced with 2-tine fork.

Above—LEMON PORK CHOPS WITH PEPPER-RICE RINGS

Harvest Pork Chops

Makes 6 servings

6 rib or shoulder pork chops, cut
 ½ inch thick
½ cup catsup
 Grated rind of ½ orange
½ cup orange juice
¼ teaspoon salt

1. Trim excess fat from chops; score fat edges 1 inch apart to keep chops from curling while cooking.
2. Brown chops well on both sides over medium heat in hot fat rendered from trimmings in large heavy frying pan with tight-fitting cover; pour off excess fat.
3. Combine catsup, orange rind and juice, and salt in small bowl; pour over

and around chops in frying pan; cover tightly.

4. Simmer, basting often, 45 minutes, or until chops are tender when pierced with 2-tine fork.

Lemon Pork Chops with Pepper-Rice Rings

Makes 4 servings

  4 loin, rib, or shoulder pork chops, cut
    ¾ inch thick
  ½ teaspoon paprika
  ½ teaspoon salt (for chops)
  ⅛ teaspoon pepper
  ½ cup raw rice
  1 medium-size onion, peeled
  4 thin slices lemon
  1 large green pepper, cut crosswise
    into 4 rings
2¼ cups (1 pint, 2-ounce can) tomato juice
  2 teaspoons sugar
  1 teaspoon salt (for sauce)
  ½ teaspoon chili powder
  1 bay leaf, finely crushed

1. Trim excess fat from chops; score fat edges 1 inch apart to keep chops from curling while cooking; sprinkle chops with paprika, salt (for chops), and pepper.

2. Brown chops well on both sides over medium heat in hot fat rendered from trimmings in large heavy frying pan with tight-fitting cover; pour off any excess fat.

3. Cook rice 5 minutes in boiling salted water while chops brown; drain.

4. Cut 1 quarter-inch slice from center of onion; separate into rings; chop remaining onion; combine with rice in medium-size bowl; save for Step 6.

5. Place lemon slice and onion ring on each chop.

6. Arrange green pepper rings around chops; fill rings with rice-onion mixture.

7. Combine tomato juice, sugar, salt

(for sauce), chili powder, and bay leaf in small bowl; pour enough liquid over chops in pan to make depth of ¼ inch; cover tightly.

8. Simmer 1 hour, or until chops are tender when pierced with 2-tine fork and rice is cooked. (Add remaining tomato-chili mixture as needed to keep liquid ¼-inch deep during cooking.)

9. Place chops on heated platter; garnish with rice-stuffed pepper rings; spoon tomato sauce over chops and rice.

Pork-Chop Potato Scallop

Bake at 350° F about 1 hour . . . .
Makes 4 servings

  4 shoulder, loin, or rib pork chops, cut
    ½ inch thick
  4 cups thinly sliced pared uncooked
    potatoes (about 5 medium-size)
  1 large onion, sliced
2½ tablespoons **Seasoned Flour,**
    page 41
  1 can condensed cream of mushroom
    soup
    Salt and pepper
    Paprika

1. Trim excess fat from chops; score fat edges 1 inch apart to keep chops from curling while cooking.

2. Brown chops well on both sides over medium heat in hot fat rendered from trimmings in large heavy frying pan; save for Step 4.

3. Layer half the potatoes, onion slices, SEASONED FLOUR, and soup in well-greased 2-quart baking dish; repeat with remaining half of ingredients.

4. Place browned chops on top; sprinkle lightly with salt and pepper, generously with paprika; cover tightly.

5. Bake in moderate oven (350°F) 1 hour, or until chops and potatoes are tender when pierced with 2-tine fork.

Stuffed Pork Chops

Makes 4 servings

4 rib or loin pork chops, cut 1 inch thick
   Apple-Raisin Stuffing, page 140
3 tablespoons flour
½ teaspoon dry mustard
½ teaspoon salt
¼ teaspoon pepper
1 small onion, sliced
¼ cup water

Cut deep pockets (below) in 1-inch rib chops along top of bone, or make pockets in loin chops by cutting from the fat edge.

Pack stuffing in pockets (about ½ cup in each); fasten openings with wooden picks; rub the chops well with SEASONED FLOUR.

1. Trim excess fat from chops; score fat edges 1 inch apart to keep chops from curling while cooking.
2. Make deep pocket for stuffing in rib chop by cutting into meat along or between rib bones with sharp short-bladed knife. Make pocket for stuffing in loin chop by cutting into meat along outside fat edge of chop.
3. Fill pockets with APPLE-RAISIN STUFFING; close openings with wooden picks (see photographs at left).
4. Combine flour, mustard, salt, and pepper in pie plate; rub into both sides of chops; save remaining flour mixture for gravy.
5. Brown chops well on both sides over medium heat in hot fat rendered from trimmings in large heavy frying pan with tight-fitting cover; pour off any excess fat.
6. Place onion slices on top of chops; add water; cover tightly.
7. Simmer 1 hour, or until chops are tender when pierced with 2-tine fork.
8. Place chops and onion rings on heated platter; remove wooden picks; keep hot.
9. Make gravy following directions, page 133, using flour left over in Step 4. Add more flour, if needed.

Pork Roasts

To Buy Buy loin end, center cut, or rib end of the pork loin, tenderloin, shoulder butt (Boston butt), picnic shoulder, crown roast, or "fresh ham" (pork leg) for roasting. The *loin end* contains the tenderloin.

The *tenderloin* (weighing ¾ to 1½ pounds) is sometimes sold separately whole or cut and flattened into fillets. *Picnics* and *shoulder butts* may be bought bone-in or boned. *Pork legs* (fresh ham) are sold bone-in or boned and are usually cut into smaller roasts. *Pork crown roast* is made from the rib end of the loin.

Crown roast   *Loin roast, center cut.*   *Fresh picnic shoulder*

To Store   Wrap meat loosely in waxed paper or aluminum foil. Store in your refrigerator. Use within 4 days. Always serve pork well done. It should be gray, without a tinge of pink.

Roast Shoulder of Pork

Roast at 325° F about 3 hours ...

   4 pounds shoulder of pork, rolled
   ¼ cup **Seasoned Flour**, page 41

1. Rub meat well with SEASONED FLOUR.
2. Place meat on rack, fat side up, in open roasting pan; insert meat thermometer so bulb reaches center of cut. (Or figure the time needed according to TIMETABLE below.)
3. Do not add water. Do not cover pan.
4. Roast pork in slow oven (325° F) until thermometer registers 185° F, or for the time needed according to TIMETABLE.
5. Place meat on heated platter; keep hot.
6. Make gravy following directions, page 133.

Crown Roast of Pork

Roast at 325° F about 3½ hours ...

5½ pounds crown roast of pork (about
   12 chops)
   Bacon
   Salt and pepper
   Sweet Potato Stuffing, page 140

1. Have meatman prepare roast, removing chine bone.
2. Wrap chop bones with bacon or aluminum foil to prevent charring; place crown upright on rack in shallow roasting pan; sprinkle with salt and pepper; fill center with stuffing.
3. Insert meat thermometer so bulb reaches center of 1 pork chop. (Or figure the time needed according to TIMETABLE below.)
4. Do not add water. Do not cover pan.
5. Roast in slow oven (325° F) until thermometer registers 185° F, or for time needed according to TIMETABLE.
6. Place meat on heated platter; remove coverings from bones; keep hot.
7. Make gravy following directions, page 133.
8. Serve roast with gravy; garnish with stuffed olives, if desired.

TIMETABLE*
Fresh Pork†
Roasted at 325° F

Cut	Approx. Weight (lbs.)	Approx. Time (hours)	Meat Thermometer
Loin	2-3	1½-2	185° F
Loin	5-7	3-4	185° F
Shoulder (fresh picnic or Boston butt)	4-6	3-4	185° F
Ham	6-8	4½-5½	185° F
Crown Roast	4-6	3-4	185° F

*If boned and rolled, add 10 minutes per pound.
†Time is for chilled meat from the refrigerator.

81

Stuffed Pork Loin

Roast at 325° F about 3 hours . . .

4 pounds pork loin (about 8 chops)
Apple-Raisin Stuffing, page 140
Salt and pepper

1. Have meatman remove chine bone and cut chops almost through; allow 1 to 2 chops per serving.
2. Fill spaces between chops with APPLE-RAISIN STUFFING; fasten with skewers or tie with clean white string so stuffing remains between chops; bake any remaining stuffing in small baking dish.
3. Place meat on rack, fat side up, in shallow roasting pan; insert meat thermometer so bulb reaches center of 1 chop. (Or figure the time needed according to TIMETABLE, page 81.) Sprinkle with salt and pepper.
4. Do not add water. Do not cover.
5. Roast pork in slow oven (325°F) until thermometer registers 185°F, or for time needed according to TIMETABLE.
6. Place meat on platter; keep hot.
7. Make gravy following directions, page 133.

To roast without filling, just have chine bone removed.

Other Cuts of Pork

To Buy Hocks, side meat, and neck bones are the least expensive cuts of pork. *Shoulder hocks* are sold fresh or cured and smoked. *Spareribs* ordinarily are sold fresh but may be cured and smoked. Quality ribs have a good portion of meat between the ribs.

Fat cuts such as *pork bellies, briskets, plates, jowls,* and *fat back* are used chiefly for flavoring or are rendered into lard. *Fresh pork shoulder* is sometimes cut up for stew or ground.

To Store Wrap loosely in waxed paper or aluminum foil; store flat in your refrigerator. Use within 3 days.

Pork Stew, Castiglione

Makes 6 servings

1½ pounds fresh pork shoulder, cubed
1 tablespoon fat
1 large onion, sliced
1 clove of garlic, finely chopped
1 can (1 pound, 13 ounces) sauerkraut
1 tablespoon sugar
2 teaspoons chopped parsley
1 teaspoon caraway seeds
¼ teaspoon thyme
¼ teaspoon powdered dill
⅛ teaspoon pepper
2 cups water

1. Brown meat over medium heat in hot fat in large heavy frying pan with tight-fitting cover, or in Dutch oven; push aside in pan; saute onion and garlic over low heat 10 to 15 minutes, or just until onion is tender.
2. Stir in sauerkraut, sugar, parsley, caraway seeds, thyme, dill, pepper, and water; cover tightly.
3. Bring to boiling; reduce heat; simmer 1 hour, or until meat is tender when pierced with 2-tine fork.

Braised Hocks with Cabbage

Makes 4 servings

4 pork hocks
Salt and pepper
2 cups water
¼ cup vinegar
¼ cup brown sugar, firmly packed
1 teaspoon celery seeds
1 large onion, chopped (1 cup)
1 medium-size head (about 1½ pounds) cabbage, cut into 8 wedges

1. Trim rind from hocks; sprinkle hocks lightly with salt and pepper.
2. Brown well on all sides over medium heat in hot fat rendered from rind in large heavy frying pan with tight-fitting cover, or in Dutch oven; pour off excess fat.

3. Add water, vinegar, sugar, celery seeds, and onion; cover tightly; reduce heat.

4. Simmer, turning meat occasionally, 1½ hours, or just until meat is tender when pierced with 2-tine fork.

5. Place cabbage wedges on top of meat; cover tightly; simmer 30 minutes, or until cabbage is tender.

6. Place meat and cabbage wedges on heated platter; keep hot.

7. Make gravy following directions, page 133.

Lancaster Skillet

Makes 4 servings

1 tablespoon butter or margarine
1 pound fresh pork shoulder, cubed
1 large onion, sliced
2 cups (about 1-pound can) tomatoes
½ cup diced celery
1 teaspoon sugar
1 teaspoon salt
¼ teaspoon sage
⅛ teaspoon pepper
2 tablespoons flour
1 can (3 or 4 ounces) sliced mushrooms

1. Melt butter or margarine in medium-size frying pan with tight-fitting cover; brown meat over medium heat; push aside in pan; saute onion over low heat 10 to 15 minutes, or just until tender.

2. Stir in tomatoes, celery, sugar, salt, sage, and pepper; cover tightly.

3. Simmer 40 minutes, or until meat is almost tender.

4. Blend flour to smooth paste with liquid drained from can of mushrooms in small bowl.

5. Stir into simmering meat mixture; add mushrooms; cook until mixture thickens and boils 1 minute.

6. Simmer 8 to 10 minutes to blend flavors. Serve with rice or noodles, if desired.

BROILER-CRISP SPARERIBS

Broiler-Crisp Spareribs

Makes 4 servings

4 pounds fresh spareribs, cut into serving-size pieces
2 medium-size onions, sliced
1 tablespoon cornstarch
¼ cup water
½ cup vinegar
¼ cup catsup
¼ cup molasses
¼ cup soy sauce
1 clove of garlic, minced

1. Place ribs in large saucepan with tight-fitting cover; add onions and enough water to cover; cover tightly.

2. Bring to boiling; reduce heat; simmer 1 hour, or until meat is tender when pierced with 2-tine fork; drain.

3. Blend cornstarch to smooth paste with water in small saucepan; stir in remaining ingredients.

4. Cook over low heat, stirring constantly, until sauce thickens and boils 1 minute.

5. Place drained ribs in single layer on rack in broiler pan; brush with half the sauce.

6. Broil, with tops of ribs about 6 inches from unit or tip of flame, 10 minutes, or until crisp and brown.

7. Turn ribs; brush with remaining sauce; broil 8 to 10 minutes, or until second side is crisp.

8. Place on heated platter.

Ways with Leftover Pork...

Sweet 'n' Sour Pork
Makes 4 servings

1½ cups cubed cooked pork
   1 tablespoon fat
   1 small onion, chopped (¼ cup)
1½ tablespoons flour
   2 tablespoons brown sugar
   ½ teaspoon salt
   3 tablespoons lemon juice
   1 cup water
   1 can (about 1 pound) green beans

1. Brown meat over medium heat in hot fat in medium-size frying pan; push aside in pan; add onion; saute over low heat 5 minutes, or just until tender.
2. Combine flour, brown sugar, and salt in small bowl; stir in lemon juice and water gradually; add to meat-onion mixture.
3. Cook, stirring constantly, until mixture thickens and boils 1 minute.
4. Add beans; simmer 12 to 15 minutes, or until heated through.

Scalloped Pork and Rice
Bake at 350°F about 45 minutes . . .
Makes 4 servings

   1 tablespoon butter or margarine
   1 medium-size onion, finely chopped
     (½ cup)
   ½ cup finely chopped green pepper
   2 cups cubed cooked pork
   2 cups cooked rice
   1 can condensed cream of mushroom
     soup
   ½ cup milk
   ½ teaspoon salt
   ¼ teaspoon rosemary
   ⅛ teaspoon pepper
     Paprika

1. Melt butter or margarine in small frying pan; saute onion and green pep-per over low heat 10 to 15 minutes, or just until onion is tender.
2. Combine pork, rice, mushroom soup, milk, salt, rosemary, and pepper in large bowl; add onion and green pepper; blend thoroughly.
3. Spoon mixture into well-greased 1½-quart casserole; sprinkle top with paprika.
4. Bake in moderate oven (350°F) 45 minutes, or until hot.

Puerto Rican Meat Pies
Bake at 425°F for 25 to 30 minutes . . .
Makes 4 pies

   1 package piecrust mix
   2 tablespoons butter or margarine
   1 small onion, finely chopped (¼ cup)
1½ cups ground cooked pork
   ½ cup chili sauce
   6 large stuffed olives, finely chopped
   1 tablespoon capers
   ¼ teaspoon chili powder
   ⅛ teaspoon pepper

1. Prepare pastry according to directions on package of mix; divide pastry into 8 equal portions; roll out each portion on lightly floured pastry cloth or board into a 4½-inch round; place each round on piece of waxed paper; chill while preparing filling.
2. Melt butter or margarine in medium-size saucepan; saute onion over low heat 5 minutes, or just until tender; stir in pork, chili sauce, olives, capers, chili powder, and pepper.
3. Simmer over low heat 5 to 8 minutes; cool slightly.
4. Divide filling into 4 equal portions; spoon 1 portion (about ½ cup) on each of 4 rounds; top with remaining rounds; pinch edges together to seal with fingers or by pressing with tines of fork; prick top; place on ungreased cooky sheet.
5. Bake in hot oven (425°F) 25 to 30 minutes, or until pastry is lightly browned.

Ham

Ham Steaks

Smoked ham: shank half　　　*Smoked ham: butt half*

To Buy For broiling, pan-broiling, or baking, buy a slice cut from center of ready-to-eat or fully cooked ham or picnic. For broiling or baking, buy slices ½ to 2 inches thick; for pan-broiling (also referred to as pan-frying, since meat does fry in its own fat) buy slices ¼ to 1 inch thick. *Uncooked* ham and picnic slices can be braised like pork steaks.

To Store Wrap in waxed paper or aluminum foil; keep in your refrigerator; use within 1 week.

Honey-Broiled Ham and Peaches

Makes 6 to 8 servings

> 2 slices ready-to-eat ham, cut ½ inch thick
> Ground cloves
> ¾ cup honey
> 1 can (1 pound, 13 ounces) peach halves
> Whole cloves

1. Score fat on ham slices to prevent curling while broiling; lightly sprinkle meat with ground cloves.
2. Place ham slices on rack in broiler pan; spread tops with about ¼ cup honey; save rest of honey for Step 5.
3. Broil, with top of ham 4 inches from unit or tip of flame, 5 minutes, or until brown and glazed.
4. Drain syrup from peaches while ham broils; stud each peach half with 2 or 3 whole cloves.
5. Turn ham slices; place peaches, rounded side up, on broiler rack; dribble rest of honey over ham and peaches.
6. Broil 5 minutes, or until meat and peaches are glazed.

Country-Fried Ham, Eggs, and Potatoes

Makes 4 servings

> 4 medium-size cold cooked potatoes, peeled and thinly sliced
> ¼ cup bacon drippings or fat
> Salt and pepper
> 4 slices ready-to-eat ham, cut about ¼ inch thick
> 4 eggs

1. Fry potatoes in hot bacon drippings or fat over low heat in large heavy frying pan, turning often, 15 minutes, or until potatoes are crisp and brown; sprinkle with salt and pepper to taste. (Add more fat during frying, if needed.)
2. Cook ham in second large heavy frying pan over medium heat until edges curl; place ham on heated platter; keep hot.
3. Melt just enough bacon drippings or fat in same frying pan to cover bottom of pan with thin film.
4. Break each egg into cup; slip into pan.
5. Cook over low heat just until whites set; cover tightly; steam eggs 3 or 4 minutes; sprinkle with salt and pepper.
6. Serve 1 slice ham, 1 egg, and 1 portion potatoes on individual plates, or arrange on large platter.

Barbecued Picnic Steaks

Makes 4 servings

    4 picnic steaks, cut ½ inch thick
    2 tablespoons flour
    ½ cup chili sauce
    1 small onion, chopped (¼ cup)
    1 tablespoon vinegar
    2 teaspoons prepared mustard
    1 teaspoon sugar
    ⅛ teaspoon pepper

1. Score fat on steaks to prevent curling while cooking; dust both sides with flour.
2. Brown steaks over medium heat on both sides in hot fat rendered from trimmings in large heavy frying pan with tight-fitting cover.
3. Blend remaining ingredients in small bowl.
4. Pour off fat in frying pan; pour chili-sauce mixture over meat; cover tightly.
5. Simmer 30 to 35 minutes, or until meat is tender when pierced with 2-tine fork.
6. Place meat on heated platter; spoon remaining sauce over steaks. Serve with hot buttered rice, if desired.

Hams—
Whole and Half

To Buy   New ways of curing and smoking ham give you tender mild meat that requires no overnight soaking and no long simmering. There are many types to choose from and the cooking method for each varies, so it is important to know which one you are buying. All hams from U. S. Government-inspected plants bear the stamp "U. S. Inspected and Passed."

Hams are sold *whole* (ranging in weight from 8 to 18 pounds), *half* (*butt* and *shank* ends), and by the slice (center cut). *Butt* halves sell for a higher price than *shank* halves because they contain less bone. *Short shank* or *shankless* hams sell at a higher price than those with shank.

Hams are available bone-in or boned and are sold as "fully cooked", "ready-to-eat", uncooked, "Tennessee or Country Style", "Smithfield" or "Virginia" style, and canned. Packers identify the quality of their products by brand names. The type of ham you buy depends upon the size of your family, the amount of time you have to prepare it, and the flavor you like.

Here are the types of ham you'll find at most meat counters, and directions for storing and baking each.

Uncooked (Cook-Before-Eating) Ham
This popular ham is cured and smoked in a special way to give it a mild delicious flavor. After a lazy baking and a quick glazing, it's all ready to serve. However, unlike the old-style heavily cured kind, this ham *must* be kept in the refrigerator both before and after baking. Use within 2 weeks. Bake according to directions on the wrapper, or as follows: Place whole or half ham, fat side up, in uncovered baking pan. Bake according to the TIMETABLE, page 88. One-half hour before ham is done, remove from oven; skin; score fat; stud with cloves; glaze, following directions, page 89.

Cooked (Ready-to-Eat) Ham   This ham has had the same mild curing and smoking as the Uncooked (Cook-Before-Eating) ham we have just described and it, too, should be stored in the refrigerator at all times. Use within 1 week. It may be served cold, without any cooking, or you may prefer to heat and glaze it to serve hot. Heat this ham

Right—HONEY-BROILED HAM AND PEACHES,
page 85

according to directions on the wrapper, or as follows: Place whole or half ham, fat side up, in uncovered baking pan. Do not add water. Bake according to TIMETABLE, below. One-half hour before ham is done, remove from oven; skin; score fat; stud with cloves; glaze, following directions, page 89.

Country-Style and Tennessee Hams
These are old-style hams, heavily cured and smoked. They keep well in a cool place for several months, and need no refrigeration. However, because of the heavy cure, they must be soaked and then simmered until tender. Here's how to do it: Place the whole ham in large kettle with tight-fitting cover; cover with cold water; soak overnight.

Next day, drain; then cover with fresh water; cover tightly. Bring to boiling; reduce heat; simmer 4 to 5 hours, or until tender. Drain; skin; score fat; stud with cloves; glaze, following directions, page 89.

Virginia and Smithfield-Type Hams
These are aged for varying periods up to 18 months. Scrub thoroughly with a stiff brush and warm water to remove layer of pepper cure. Then soak overnight and cook following directions for COUNTRY-STYLE HAM.

Canned Ham Canned hams vary in weight from 1½ pounds to a full-size ham. All canned hams (except the 1½-pound ham) must be kept in the re-

TIMETABLE
Hams†
Baked at 325° F

	Approx. Weight (lbs.)	Approx. Time (hours)	Meat Thermometer
Whole, Uncooked (cook-before-eating)	10-15	3-5	170° F
Half, Uncooked (cook-before-eating)	5-7	2¼-3	170° F
	8-10	3½-4	170° F
Whole, Cooked (ready-to-eat)	10-12	2-2½	160° F
	12-15	2½-3	160° F
	15-18	3-3½	160° F
Half, Cooked (ready-to-eat)	5-8	1½	160° F
	8-10	2	160° F
Picnic			
Uncooked (cook-before-eating)	4-7	2½-3¾	170° F
	8-10	4-5	170° F
Cooked (ready-to-eat)	4-6	1¼	160° F
	7-10	1¾	160° F
Shoulder Butt			
Uncooked (cook-before-eating)	2-4	1½-2⅓	170° F

†Time is for chilled meat from the refrigerator.

Score fat into diamonds (or squares) using a string-and-wooden-pick guide to make cuts straight. Stud with cloves, if desired.

Spread glaze (see glazes, below) evenly over top of ham; bake, basting often, 30 minutes, or until the ham is shiny and glazed.

frigerator. The 1½-pound ham is specially canned so it may be kept on the pantry shelf. But check the label to be sure.

Canned ham is ready to eat cold or hot. To heat, remove ham from can; place in shallow baking pan. Heat in moderate oven (350°F) 15 to 20 minutes per pound. (Time is for chilled ham right out of the refrigerator.) If desired, stud with cloves and glaze, following directions below.

Prosciutto Ham This is a partially boned, lean ham that is given a long dry cure and smoked according to methods originated in Italy. It need not be cooked before eating.

How To Glaze Baked Ham

One-half hour before ham is done, remove from oven. Take off skin by holding it with a fork, pliers, or kitchen tongs and cutting it away from fat with sharp knife. Score fat in squares or diamonds with sharp knife. Leave top plain or stud with whole cloves. Pour drippings from baking pan. Cover ham with one of the glazes described at right. (Amounts given are enough for a whole ham; halve these for picnic or half of ham.) Bake in slow oven (325°F) 30 minutes, or until top is shiny and glazed, and ham or picnic is tender when pierced with 2-tine fork.

Suggested Glazes

1 cup sifted brown sugar mixed with 2 tablespoons flour and 1 tablespoon dry mustard. Sift over top to spread evenly.

4 tablespoons prepared mustard and 1 cup corn syrup. Spread mustard on ham; pour over syrup; baste several times.

1 cup currant jelly melted in ¼ cup hot water. Spoon over ham; baste several times with jelly mixture in bottom of pan.

1 cup orange or apricot marmalade, heated until marmalade melts. Spoon over ham; baste several times.

1 cup brown sugar mixed with 2 tablespoons prepared mustard and 6 tablespoons vinegar. Spoon over ham; baste several times.

1 cup peach or pineapple preserves mixed with ½ teaspoon ground cloves, heated until preserves melt. Spoon over ham; baste several times.

1 cup honey. Drizzle over top of ham; baste often.

> *Freezing ham is not recommended, since the fat of salted meats may become rancid when frozen.*

Garnishes for Hams

Press a maraschino-cherry half in the center of each square or diamond of a marmalade-glazed ham. Glaze will keep cherries in place.

Decorate a honey-glazed ham with flowers made with halved seedless grapes and maraschino-cherry halves. Glaze will keep decorations in place.

Decorate peach-glazed ham with jelly-bean flowers, using jelly beans halved crosswise for centers, and halved lengthwise for petals. Press onto hot ham. Glaze will keep them in place.

For a party ham, glaze ham with honey; decorate at once with flowers made of halved seedless grapes and maraschino cherries (glaze keeps decorations in place).

*Shoulder butt
Picnic*

Picnic and Boneless Butt

To Buy *Picnics,* cut from shoulders, are cured and smoked to give you the same flavor as ham for less cost. They are also known as *picnic hams* and *callies.* The bone is small and there should be little fat.

Some picnics are marked "ready-to-eat" and may be served as is, or heated in a slow oven (325°F), allowing about 10 minutes per pound. Other picnics are uncooked and marked "cook-before-eating." Either bake and glaze these, or simmer in water and then glaze them. Buy a whole picnic to bake or simmer, or, if your family is small, have your meatman cut one into 3 parts.

Smoked boneless butt or *shoulder butt* is made by boning the blade section of a pork shoulder. It is also known as *cottage butt* and *cottage roll.* Picnics and boneless butts are low cost and excellent buys for small families.

Orange-Glaze Picnic Roast

To bake and glaze an uncooked picnic: Wrap a 4- to 8-pound smoked picnic loosely in its inner wrapper or in clean wrapping paper. Place, fat side up, on rack in baking pan. Do not add water. Do not cover. Bake according to the TIMETABLE, page 88. One-half hour befor picnic is done, remove from wrapping; glaze with orange marmalade following directions, page 89.

To simmer and glaze an uncooked picnic: Place 4- to 8-pound smoked picnic in large kettle with tight-fitting cover; cover with water; cover tightly; bring to boiling; reduce heat; simmer, allowing 35 to 45 minutes per pound, until tender when pierced with 2-tine fork. Remove from water; cut away rind with sharp knife. Season; score top; glaze with orange marmalade following directions, page 89.

Baked Stuffed Picnic

Bake at 325° F about 3¼ hours

- 1 smoked picnic (about 5 pounds)
- 1 package ready-mix bread stuffing
  Whole cloves
- 1 cup brown sugar, firmly packed
- 1 tablespoon vinegar
- 1 teaspoon dry mustard
- 1 can (about 1 pound) peach halves,
  drained
  Parsley

1. Have picnic boned to make pocket for stuffing; cut off rind, removing as little fat as possible.

2. Prepare stuffing according to directions on package.

3. Fill pocket with stuffing; fasten with skewers.

4. Place, fat side up, on rack in baking pan.

5. Do not add water. Do not cover.

6. Bake following TIMETABLE, page 88.

7. One-half hour before picnic is done remove from oven; glaze with sugar-vinegar-mustard mixture, following directions, page 89.

8. Place meat on heated platter; remove skewers; garnish platter with peach halves and parsley.

Below—HAM LOAF, *page 93*, and STUFFED APRICOTS, *page 138*

Easy Picnic Bake

Bake at 325°F about 1½ hours . . .
Makes 3 to 4 servings

Place butt end (about 2 pounds, cut from 6- to 8-pound uncooked picnic ham), cut side down, on rack in baking pan. Do not add water. Do not cover pan. Bake according to TIMETABLE, page 88. One-half hour before picnic is done, remove from oven; glaze following directions, page 89.

Country-Style Ham and Sauerkraut Dinner

Makes 3 to 4 servings

    1 picnic hock, split in half (about 1½ pounds)
    1 can (1 pound, 13 ounces) sauerkraut, drained
    1 cup water
    1 large apple, pared, cored, and sliced
    1 medium-size onion, chopped (½ cup)
    2 tablespoons brown sugar
    ¼ cup vinegar
    1 tablespoon butter or margarine
    8 small (about 1 pound) potatoes, washed but not pared
    Salt and pepper

1. Combine picnic hock, sauerkraut, water, apple, onion, sugar, vinegar, and butter or margarine in large saucepan; cover tightly.
2. Bring to boiling; reduce heat; simmer 1½ to 2 hours, or until hock is almost tender, stirring occasionally to blend ingredients and to prevent sticking.
3. Add potatoes; simmer about ½ hour, or until potatoes and hock are tender when pierced with 2-tine fork.
4. Season to taste with salt and pepper.

Ways with Leftover Ham . . .

Seven-Layer Casserole

Bake at 350°F about 1 hour . . .
Makes 6 servings

    8 **Thin Pancakes,** page 136
    1½ cups finely chopped cooked ham
    1 can (1 pound, 4 ounces) asparagus spears, drained
    2 cups (about ½ pound) grated process American cheese
    2 eggs, slightly beaten
    ½ cup milk
    ½ cup thick sour cream

1. Prepare THIN PANCAKES.
2. Place 1 pancake in bottom of greased 2-quart casserole; cover with thin sprinkling of ham; arrange a few spears of asparagus over ham; top with thin sprinkling of cheese; repeat to make 6 layers, using all ham, asparagus, and cheese; top with remaining pancake.
3. Blend eggs and milk in small bowl; pour over layers; cover tightly.
4. Bake in moderate oven (350°F) 1 hour, or until custard is set.
5. Serve in casserole; garnish with sour cream.

SEVEN-LAYER CASSEROLE

Fruited Ham Loaf

Bake at 350°F about 1 hour . . .
Makes 6 servings

4 cups ground cooked ham
1 cup (about 2 slices) soft bread
crumbs
½ cup catsup
3 eggs
1 large onion, finely chopped (1 cup)
1 teaspoon dry mustard
¼ teaspoon ground cloves
Stuffed Apricots, page 138
Parsley

1. Combine ham, bread crumbs, catsup, eggs, onion, mustard, and cloves in large bowl; toss together lightly with 2-tine fork.
2. Pack mixture into greased loaf pan, 9x5x3.
3. Bake in moderate oven (350°F) 1 hour, or until center of loaf is firm.
4. Place loaf on heated platter; garnish top with 3 apricot halves, if desired; arrange STUFFED APRICOTS and parsley around loaf.

Ham Tamale Pie

Bake at 375°F about 25 minutes . . .
Makes 6 servings

1 large onion, chopped (1 cup)
½ small green pepper, chopped
1 clove of garlic, minced
2 tablespoons salad or olive oil
1 tablespoon flour
2 teaspoons chili powder
2 cups diced cooked ham
1 can (12 ounces) vacuum-pack
whole-kernel corn
2¼ cups (1-pint, 2-ounce can) tomato
juice
¼ cup seedless raisins
1 package corn-muffin mix
⅔ cup milk

1. Saute onion, green pepper, and garlic over low heat in hot oil in large heavy frying pan 10 to 15 minutes, or until onion is tender.
2. Blend in flour and chili powder; stir in ham, corn, tomato juice, and raisins; cook until heated through.
3. Blend corn-muffin mix with milk in medium-size bowl while ham mixture heats; pour ham mixture into baking dish, 12x8x2; spoon batter around edge to make a border.
4. Bake in moderate oven (375°F) 25 minutes, or until topping is golden brown.

Ham Croquettes

Makes 8 croquettes

2 cups coarsely ground cooked ham
1 cup (about 2 slices) soft bread
crumbs
2 eggs, well-beaten
1 tablespoon milk (for croquettes)
1 tablespoon minced onion
1 tablespoon finely chopped green
pepper
1 teaspoon chili powder
½ cup fine dry bread crumbs
½ cup milk (for coating)
Melted vegetable shortening, lard, or
salad oil to make 4-inch depth in
kettle, or depth in electric fryer
following manufacturer's directions

1. Combine ham, soft bread crumbs, eggs, milk (for croquettes), onion, green pepper, and chili powder in medium-size bowl; chill about 2 hours.
2. Shape into 8 croquettes; roll each in dry bread crumbs; dip in milk (for coating); roll again in crumbs; remove any loose crumbs.
3. Heat fat in deep heavy kettle to 365°F–375°F (a 1-inch cube of bread will brown in about 60 seconds).
4. Fry croquettes, 3 or 4 at a time, 2 to 3 minutes, or until golden brown; drain on absorbent paper.
5. Serve on heated platter with hot TOMATO SAUCE, page 130, if desired.

Red Flannel Hash

Makes 6 generous servings

    2 cups lean cooked ham
    4 peeled, cooked medium-size potatoes
    1 can (about 1 pound) sliced beets, drained
    1 large onion, quartered
    2 tablespoons vinegar
    2 teaspoons sugar
    ½ teaspoon salt
    ¼ teaspoon pepper
    2 tablespoons fat

1. Put ham, potatoes, beets, and onion through food chopper, using perforated coarse plate.
2. Stir vinegar, sugar, salt, and pepper into mixture in large bowl.
3. Heat fat in large heavy frying pan with tight-fitting cover; add hash mixture; cover tightly.
4. Heat slowly to give hash a brown crust on bottom.
5. Uncover; slide hash in frying pan under broiler; broil, with top of hash 3 inches from unit or tip of flame, 2 to 3 minutes to brown top.

Chinese Fried Rice

Makes 4 servings

    ½ cup diced cooked ham or pork
    1 can (3 or 4 ounces) sliced mushrooms
    1 medium-size onion, chopped (½ cup)
    2 tablespoons soy sauce
    4 cups cold cooked rice (about 1 cup raw)
    2 tablespoons salad oil
    1 egg, well beaten

1. Combine meat, mushrooms, onion, soy sauce, rice, and salad oil in large heavy frying pan.
2. Cook over low heat, stirring often, 10 minutes; blend in egg; cook, stirring constantly, 5 minutes.
3. Serve on heated platter.

Link sausages crisp and brown make a wonderful breakfast with tender pancakes.

Ham Hawaiian

Makes 4 servings

    2 tablespoons butter or margarine
    1 teaspoon curry powder
    1 cup diced celery
    1 medium-size onion, chopped (½ cup)
    1 green pepper, cut in thin strips
    1 tablespoon cornstarch
    1 can (9 ounces) pineapple tidbits
    ½ cup orange juice
    2 cups cooked ham, cut in thin strips
    ¼ cup slivered blanched almonds*

1. Melt butter or margarine in large heavy frying pan; add curry powder, celery, onion, and green pepper; saute over low heat 10 minutes, or until vegetables are almost tender; blend in cornstarch.
2. Drain syrup from pineapple; add water to make 1 cup; stir measured liquid, pineapple, and orange juice into mixture in frying pan.
3. Cook, stirring constantly, until sauce thickens and boils 1 minute.
4. Add ham and almonds; simmer 2 to 3 minutes to heat through.
5. Serve with seasoned, hot, cooked rice, and with shredded coconut, if desired.

*See page 141.

Sausage

To Buy Fresh and smoked pork sausage is sold in bulk, packaged in patty form, and in casings (linked or unlinked), or as skinless links. It is usually ground fine. *Country* style is coarsely ground and sold in 8- to 10-inch links, in unlinked casings, or in bulk. Fresh pork sausage is also sold precooked (ready to brown) and frozen. Smoked country-style sausage, smoked pure pork sausage, and Polish-style sausage are similar, but Polish-style sausage contains garlic.

To Store Fresh sausage is perishable and should be stored in your refrigerator. Use within 3 days. It may be frozen and kept about 1 month.

To Cook Like your link sausage plump, cooked through, and crisp on the outside? Place sausages in cold frying pan with tight-fitting cover; add about ¼ cup cold water; cover tightly; steam 5 minutes, or just until plump; remove cover; pour off any remaining water. Fry sausages over low heat, turning often by rolling sausages over, 8 to 10 minutes, or until brown and crisp. (Do not use fork for turning, since holes in the skin let juices out.) Pour off any fat as it cooks out.

Three-Decker Patties

Bake at 350°F about 40 minutes ...
Makes 6 servings

    2 large baking apples, washed and
        cored
    2 cups mashed cooked sweet potatoes
        (about 2 medium-size)
    1 teaspoon salt
    ⅛ teaspoon pepper
    1 pound pork sausage meat

1. Cut each apple into 3 thick crosswise slices; place in large shallow baking pan.

2. Blend sweet potatoes, salt, and pepper in medium-size bowl; shape into 6 thick patties the same size as apple slices; place on top of apple slices.
3. Shape sausage into 6 patties; place on top of sweet-potato patties.
4. Bake in moderate oven (350°F) 40 minutes, or until apple rings are tender when pierced with 2-tine fork and sausage is cooked (no pink remains).
5. Remove patties from pan with slotted pancake turner to allow drippings to drain off.

Rice and Sausage Bake

Bake at 375°F about 1 hour ...
Makes 4 servings

    1 pound pork sausage meat
    2 cups (about 1-pound can) tomatoes
    ¼ cup catsup
    1 small onion, finely chopped (¼ cup)
    2 teaspoons sugar
    1 teaspoon salt
    Dash of pepper
    ½ teaspoon Worcestershire sauce
    1 cup raw rice
    1½ cups water

1. Brown sausage over low heat in small frying pan, breaking up meat with 2-tine fork as it cooks; drain off all fat.
2. Combine 3 tablespoons sausage fat, tomatoes, catsup, onion, sugar, salt, pepper, and Worcestershire sauce in medium-size bowl.
3. Spread half the rice in bottom of well-greased 1½-quart baking dish; cover with half the tomato mixture and half the cooked sausage.
4. Repeat layers, using remaining ingredients; add water; cover tightly.
5. Bake in moderate oven (375°F) 1 hour, or until rice is tender and liquid is absorbed. Stir once during baking.

Sausage Puff

Bake at 350°F about 45 minutes...
Makes 6 servings

1 pound pork sausage meat
3 cups milk
1 teaspoon salt
½ cup corn meal
3 eggs, separated
¾ cup (3 ounces) grated process
   American cheese

1. Brown sausage over low heat in large heavy frying pan, breaking up meat with 2-tine fork as it cooks; drain off all fat; drain meat on absorbent paper; save for Steps 4 and 5; return 1 tablespoon fat to frying pan.
2. Scald milk in same frying pan; blend in salt and corn meal; cook over low heat, stirring constantly, until mixture thickens.
3. Beat egg whites until stiff but not dry in medium-size bowl.
4. Beat egg yolks until thick and lemon colored in large bowl; slowly stir in corn-meal mixture and all but ¼ cup sausage; gently fold in beaten egg whites.
5. Pour mixture into well-greased 2-quart baking dish; sprinkle top with cheese and remaining ¼ cup cooked sausage.
6. Bake in moderate oven (350°F) 45 minutes, or until puffy and brown on top and center is firm.

Fry *patties* (make these 3 inches by ½ inch thick) slowly 8 to 10 minutes, or until one side is well browned; turn; fry other side additional 6 to 8 minutes. Sausage should be gray inside with no trace of pink when done. All sausage should be thoroughly cooked and drained before it is eaten.

Bacon

To Buy Good bacon has a thin rind and white fat alternating with layers of meat. The flavor varies with the brand, so find the one you like. Bacon is sold sliced in ½- and 1-pound packages and vacuum packed, or in the piece (slab bacon) with the rind on. A ½-pound package contains about 12 slices. Buy only enough to last 1 week, since bacon looses its flavor and aroma quickly. Allow 2 slices per serving.

To Store Keep bacon in its original package or wrap in waxed paper or aluminum foil. Store in the refrigerator. Do not freeze, since bacon becomes rancid if held very long in the freezer.

To Cook

TO PAN-BROIL Lay bacon slices in cold frying pan; cook slowly over very low heat, turning occasionally. (If fat smokes the flavor is changed, so keep heat low.) Drain on absorbent paper; serve immediately. For very crisp bacon, pour off fat as it cooks out.

TO BROIL Place bacon slices on broiling rack; broil, with bacon 3 inches from unit or tip of flame, about 4 minutes on each side.

TO BAKE Place bacon slices on rack in shallow baking pan; bake in moderately hot oven (400°F) 10 minutes, or until browned and crisp.

Corn-and-Bacon Cakes

Makes about 24 cakes

2 slices bacon, diced
4 large ears cooked or uncooked corn
1 egg
3 tablespoons milk
½ cup sifted flour
½ teaspoon baking powder
1 teaspoon salt

1. Fry bacon on both sides until crisp in large heavy frying pan over low

Sliced bacon   Jowl bacon square   Canadian-style bacon

heat; drain on absorbent paper; leave drippings in pan.

2. MAKE CORN PULP: Cut through middle of each row of corn kernels with sharp knife; force pulp from kernels by scraping ears with back of knife.

3. Beat egg slightly in medium-size bowl.

4. Stir in corn pulp, crisp bacon, and milk.

5. Measure flour, baking powder, and salt into sifter; sift over corn mixture; stir just until blended.

6. Drop batter by teaspoonfuls into hot bacon drippings.

7. Fry cakes over medium heat 3 to 4 minutes, or until golden brown on underside; turn; fry other side. (Add fat to keep bottom of pan covered, if needed.)

8. Serve with butter or margarine and blended maple syrup, if desired.

Texas Hominy Casserole

Bake at 375°F about 45 minutes ...
Makes 6 servings

  4 slices bacon
  6 tablespoons flour
  1 teaspoon sugar
  1 teaspoon salt
  1 teaspoon chili powder
  2 cups (about 1-pound can) tomatoes
  1 can (1 pound, 14 ounces) hominy, drained
  2 large onions, sliced
  1 cup (¼ pound) grated process American cheese

1. Fry bacon on both sides until crisp in large heavy frying pan over low heat; save for Step 3; add enough fat to pan, if needed, to make 4 tablespoons.

2. Blend in flour, sugar, salt, and chili powder; stir in tomatoes; cook, stirring constantly, until thick.

3. Layer hominy, onion slices, and tomato mixture in 2-quart baking dish; sprinkle with cheese; top with bacon slices; cover tightly.

4. Bake in moderate oven (375°F) 45 minutes.

Canadian-Style Bacon

To Buy   Canadian-style bacon is lean, boned, cured, and smoked pork loin. It is usually sold in a 2- to 4-pound piece or sliced and prepackaged. It is available sliced with or without a casing and in the piece with casing. It is branded to indicate quality. Allow 2 to 4 slices, or 2 to 4 ounces in the piece, per serving.

To Store   Keep in its original package or wrap in waxed paper or aluminum foil. Store in your refrigerator. Do not freeze. Use Canadian-style bacon within 2 weeks.

To Cook

TO PAN BROIL   Lay Canadian-style bacon slices (if bacon is in casing, remove casing) in cold frying pan; fry on both sides over very low heat.

TO BROIL   Place Canadian-style bacon slices, cut about ¼ inch thick, on broiler rack (if bacon is in casing, remove casing); broil, with bacon 3 inches from unit or tip of flame, about 4 minutes on each side.

TO BAKE   Remove casing from piece of bacon (hold under running cold water for few minutes; slip off casing); place, fat side up, on rack in open roasting pan; insert meat thermometer so bulb reaches center of piece. Bake in slow oven (325°F) 1½ hours (for 2-pound piece), 2 hours (for 4-pound piece), 3 hours (for 6-pound piece), or until meat thermometer registers 170°F. Score fat; stud with cloves; spread with pineapple jam; bake in hot oven (450°F) 10 minutes, or until brown.

Skillet Bacon 'n' Eggs

Makes 4 servings

    8 slices Canadian-style bacon
    8 eggs
    ½ cup milk
    ½ teaspoon salt
    ⅛ teaspoon pepper
    2 tablespoons butter or margarine

1.   Fry bacon on both sides in large heavy frying pan over low heat just until edges curl and bacon is lightly browned; remove from pan; keep hot; wipe out pan with paper towel.

2.   Break eggs into medium-size bowl while bacon is frying; add milk, salt, and pepper; beat with rotary beater until light and foamy.

3.   Melt butter or margarine in same frying pan; pour in egg mixture; heat very slowly, pushing eggs gently with fork or tablespoon from bottom and sides as they begin to set; cook *just* until set.

4.   Serve 2 slices of bacon with scrambled eggs on heated plates.

Pork Menus

Baked Stuffed Picnic*

Peach Halves   Brown Gravy

Kale with Lemon Butter

Baked Acorn Squashes

Celery and Carrot Sticks

Gingerbread   Lemon Sauce

Beverage

* *

Lemon Pork Chops with

Pepper-Rice Rings*

Green Beans

Carrot and Raisin Salad

Whole Wheat Bread   Butter

Sliced Peaches with Cream

Beverage

* *

Braised Hocks with Cabbage*

Parsley-Buttered Potatoes

Tomato Aspic Salad with

Cottage-Cheese Dressing

Rye Bread   Butter

Fruited Gelatin

Beverage

* *

Sausage Puff*

Buttered Peas and Carrots

Tomato and Onion Salad with

French Dressing

Hard Rolls   Butter

Baked Apples

Beverage

* *

Honey-Broiled Ham and Peaches*

Sweet Potato

Scalloped Tomatoes

Cabbage Slaw

Brown-Bread Pudding

Beverage

For recipes see index

Brains—left to right, beef, veal, pork, lamb   *Hearts—left to right, lamb, pork, veal, beef*

Variety Meats

Give your family a new taste treat—serve them one of the variety meats. Tongue, liver, kidney, heart, sweetbreads, brains, and oxtails are delicious when they are well cooked. They are packed with vitamins and minerals—and best of all—most of them are very economical.

Brains

To Buy Beef, veal or calf, lamb, and pork brains all have a delicate flavor and are equally tender. They vary in size and weight: beef brains weigh ¾ to 1 pound; veal or calf, about 8 ounces; pork, 4 ounces; and lamb, about 3 ounces. Buy 1 pound of brains for 4 servings.

To Store Brains are very delicate and perishable and should be used as soon as possible after purchasing. If frozen, store in freezer or frozen-food compartment of your refrigerator. To use, cover with hot water just until thawed, then follow preparation directions below. If fresh, prepare as soon as possible. After preparing, cool, cover, and store in refrigerator. Do not store longer than 24 hours.

To Prepare Wash in cold water; soak in salted water (1 tablespoon salt to 1 quart of water) 15 minutes. Remove membrane with tip of paring knife.

Drop into boiling acidulated water (1 teaspoon salt and 1 tablespoon vinegar to 1 quart of water); cover; reduce heat; *simmer* 15 minutes (longer cooking or boiling spoils the texture). Drain; plunge into cold water; drain again.

Scrambled Eggs and Brains

Makes 4 servings

- 1 pound veal brains
- 4 eggs, unbeaten
- ¼ cup evaporated milk or cream
- 1 tablespoon chopped chives
- 1 tablespoon catsup
  Few drops of bottled hot-pepper sauce
- ¼ teaspoon salt
- 2 tablespoons butter or margarine

1. Prepare brains following directions above; break into small pieces.
2. Combine eggs, milk or cream, chives, catsup, bottled hot-pepper sauce, and salt in medium-size bowl; beat with fork just until blended; add brains.
3. Melt butter or margarine in medium-size frying pan; pour mixture into pan; cook over low heat, stirring constantly with fork and gently scraping from sides and bottom of pan as mixture begins to set, until eggs are cooked the way you like them.

Heart

To Buy Hearts are firm-textured and slightly sweet flavored. Beef hearts weigh 3 to 4 pounds and are the least tender; veal hearts weigh about 1 pound; pork ½ to 1 pound; lamb about ¼ pound. Veal and lamb hearts are the most tender. Buy hearts fresh or frozen. Fresh hearts should be clean and without odor. A beef heart makes 4 to 8 servings; veal and pork, about 2 servings; lamb, about 1 serving. Veal, pork, and lamb hearts are sometimes sold pickled in vinegar.

To Store Keep frozen hearts in freezer or frozen-food compartment of your refrigerator. Thaw in refrigerator. Store fresh hearts, loosely wrapped, in refrigerator. Use within 24 hours.

To Prepare Remove coarse fibers, veins, and arteries from heart with sharp-pointed knife or kitchen scissors; wash thoroughly in cold water.

To Cook

SIMMERED HEART Cover heart with boiling water: add 1 teaspoon salt; 1 onion, quartered; and handful of celery tops, if desired: cover tightly: simmer 1 to 2 hours, or until tender when pierced with 2-tine fork. Chop or grind the meat; substitute for lamb in BAKED HASH, page 74.

Delaware Fried Heart

Makes 4 servings

> 2 veal hearts
> Or: 4 lamb hearts
> ½ cup **Seasoned Flour**, page 41
> 2 tablespoons fat

1. Prepare hearts following directions above; drain on absorbent paper; cut into ¼-inch-thick slices.
2. Dust with SEASONED FLOUR placed in a paper bag.
3. Brown slices on both sides in hot fat in medium-size frying pan over medium heat 8 minutes, or until golden brown. Serve plain or with FLORENTINE SAUCE, page 129, if desired.

Braised Heart

Bake at 275°F about 2 hours . . .
Makes 4 to 6 servings

> 1 beef heart
> Or: 2 veal hearts
> **Bread and Butter Stuffing**, page 140
> ¼ cup **Seasoned Flour**, page 41
> 3 tablespoons fat

1. Prepare heart following directions at left; drain on absorbent paper.
2. Fill cavity with stuffing; sew or skewer opening together.
3. Roll in SEASONED FLOUR.
4. Brown on all sides in hot fat in Dutch oven over medium heat; add boiling water to depth of 1 inch; cover tightly.
5. Bake in very slow oven (275°F) 2 hours, or until heart is tender when pierced with 2-tine fork.
6. Drain; remove thread or skewer; slice; serve on heated platter with SPANISH SAUCE, page 129, if desired.

Kidney

To Buy Kidneys are prized for their distinctive flavor. Beef, lamb, and veal kidneys are favorites; pork kidneys are very low in cost, but are not always found in grocery markets or meat stores. Beef kidneys weigh about 1 pound. They vary in color from yellowish to almost black. The best are mahogany in color and are plump and firm. They should be braised or simmered. Veal kidneys weigh 5 to 12 ounces; lamb kidneys weigh about 2 ounces. Veal and lamb may be broiled or sauteed. Buy 1 pound of kidney for 4 servings.

To Store Keep, loosely wrapped, in your refrigerator for no longer than 24 hours.

To Prepare Wash in cold water; remove outer membrane; split through center lengthwise; remove white membranes and tubes with tip of sharp knife or scissors; soak in cold salted water (1 tablespoon salt to 1 quart of water) 30 minutes; drain; rinse; drain.

Sauteed Onions and Kidney

Makes 4 servings

    1 beef kidney
    1 large onion, sliced
    2 tablespoons butter or margarine
    ½ teaspoon salt
    ⅛ teaspoon pepper

1. Prepare kidney following directions above; cut into ¼-inch-thick slices; dry on absorbent paper.
2. Melt butter or margarine in medium-size frying pan with tight-fitting cover; saute onion over low heat 10 to 15 minutes, or just until tender.
3. Add kidney, salt, and pepper; brown on both sides; cover tightly.
4. Simmer 5 minutes, or until kidney is tender. Serve on toast points, if desired.

Broiled Kidneys, Marinade

Makes 4 servings

    10 lamb kidneys
    6 tablespoons vinegar
    3 tablespoons salad or olive oil
    1 teaspoon sugar
    ½ teaspoon salt
    ¼ teaspoon paprika
    ⅛ teaspoon pepper
    ⅛ teaspoon sage
    Dash of thyme
    Dash of cayenne

1. Prepare kidneys following directions, at left.
2. Combine remaining ingredients in medium-size bowl.
3. Marinate kidney halves in vinegar mixture ½ hour.
4. Place kidneys in shallow baking pan or glass pie plate; pour in enough marinade to cover bottom of pan or plate.
5. Broil, with top of meat 4 inches from unit or tip of flame, 4 minutes; turn each kidney half; broil an additional 4 minutes, or until brown. Serve on toast, if desired.

Kidney Kabobs

Makes 4 servings

    4 lamb kidneys
    2 firm tomatoes, quartered
    8 small mushrooms
    4 bacon slices, cut in half crosswise
    Salad oil
    Salt and pepper

1. Prepare kidneys following directions, above.
2. Alternate kidney halves, tomato quarters, mushrooms, and bacon, starting and ending with bacon on a 6-inch skewer; repeat to fill 4 skewers.
3. Brush with salad oil; sprinkle with salt and pepper.
4. Broil, with top of meat 4 inches from unit or tip of flame, 4 minutes; turn; broil an additional 4 minutes, or until bacon is crisp and kidneys are done.

Kidneys—left to right, veal, beef, lamb, pork

Split each kidney; cut out suet and thin white tubes with sharp knife or scissors.

Liver—left to right, beef, veal, pork, and lamb. Remove all tubes before cooking.

Beef Kidney Stew

Makes 4 generous servings

    2 beef kidneys
    3 tablespoons butter or margarine
    1 medium-size green pepper, chopped
 1½ cups hot water
    2 beef-bouillon cubes
    ½ teaspoon salt
    ½ teaspoon celery salt
    ¼ teaspoon sage
    ¼ teaspoon marjoram
      Dash of pepper
    4 carrots, peeled and quartered
    8 small white onions, peeled
    3 tablespoons flour
    ½ cup cold water

1. Prepare kidneys following directions, page 101; cut into 1-inch cubes.
2. Melt butter or margarine in Dutch oven; saute green pepper over low heat 10 to 15 minutes, or just until tender; add kidneys; saute 3 minutes, or until light brown.
3. Stir hot water, bouillon cubes, salt, celery salt, sage, marjoram, and pepper into kidney mixture; add carrots and onions; cover tightly.
4. Bring to boiling; reduce heat; simmer 30 minutes, or until vegetables and kidney are tender when pierced with 2-tine fork.
5. Blend flour to smooth paste with cold water in small bowl; stir several tablespoons hot liquid from stew into flour-water mixture; stir into stew.
6. Cook, stirring constantly, until mixture thickens and boils 1 minute.

Liver

To Buy Beef, veal, calf, pork, and lamb livers are all excellent sources of iron, copper, and vitamins—especially vitamin A, riboflavin; niacin, and thiamine (parts of the B-complex). Ounce for ounce, no other food supplies as much nutrition as liver. Because of their flavor and tenderness, veal and calf liver are the most popular—and the most expensive. Lamb liver is also tender and delicate in flavor. Beef and pork livers are stronger in flavor and less tender, but all liver can be cooked so that it is appetizing.

A whole beef liver weighs about 10 pounds; veal, calf, and pork liver about 3 pounds; and lamb about 1 pound. Buy 1 pound of any of these for 4 servings. Lighter colored beef liver is usually more tender than that of darker color. Veal liver comes from milk-fed animals and is slightly more tender than calves' livers. The latter come from older calves or from calves not fed on milk. Both, however, are usually called calves' liver. Liver should be fresh, of a clear color, and stamped to indicate U.S. Government or local inspection.

To Store If frozen, store in your freezer or the frozen-food compartment of your refrigerator. Thaw in refrigerator before cooking. If fresh, wrap loosely in waxed paper (if prepackaged, loosen wrappings) and store in the coldest part of your refrigerator not longer than 24 hours. Liver, like all variety meats, is perishable and should be used as soon as possible after purchase.

To Prepare Cut out tubes and white membrane with sharp-pointed knife or kitchen scissors; pull off skin (this toughens during cooking). Do not soak or scald liver. Precook it only when it is to be ground. Pan-fry or broil veal, calf, or lamb liver; braise pork liver; pan-fry or braise beef liver.

To Cook

TO PAN-FRY Sprinkle 1 pound liver, sliced, with SEASONED FLOUR, page 41. Brown in just enough hot fat, butter, or margarine to cover bottom of medium-size frying pan. Fry gently, over low heat, 2 to 4 minutes, or until brown on underside; turn; add more fat, if needed; brown second side. Test for doneness: Cut slash about ¾-inch long into thick part of slice; separate cut with tip of knife (if medium-done, liver is faint pink in center of cut; if well-done, liver has lost all pinkness). Overcooking makes liver tough, hard, dry, and tasteless.

TO BROIL Brush both sides of 1 pound of liver slices with melted bacon drippings, butter, or margarine; place slices on broiler pan or in shallow baking pan. Broil, with top of liver 4 inches from unit or tip of flame, 2 to 4 minutes, or until lightly browned; turn; broil other side. Use same test for doneness as for pan-fried liver.

TO BRAISE (pork or beef) Sprinkle 1 pound liver, sliced, with SEASONED FLOUR, page 41. Brown in just enough hot fat, butter, or margarine to cover bottom of medium-size frying pan. Fry gently, over low heat, 2 to 4 minutes, or until brown on underside; turn; add more fat if needed; brown second side. Add 1½ cups tomato juice, stock, or water; simmer 30 minutes, or until tender when pierced with 2-tine fork.

Savory Liver and Sausage Bake

Bake at 350°F about 45 minutes . . . Makes 6 to 8 servings

1 pound beef liver
2 tablespoons butter or margarine
1 medium-size onion, coarsely chopped (½ cup)
½ cup finely diced celery
3 shredded wheat biscuits
½ cup (about 1 slice) coarse soft bread crumbs
½ pound pork sausage meat
¼ cup chili sauce
2 eggs, well beaten
1 tablespoon lemon juice
1 teaspoon salt
1 teaspoon Worcestershire sauce
½ teaspoon marjoram
⅛ teaspoon pepper
2 slices bacon, cut in quarters crosswise

1. Prepare liver following directions, at left.
2. Cover liver with boiling water in medium-size saucepan; simmer 5 minutes; drain; cool.
3. Melt butter or margarine in same saucepan; saute onion and celery over low heat 10 minutes, or just until onion is tender; save for Step 5.
4. Chop cooked liver coarsely with knife, or grind using coarse perforated plate; place in large bowl.
5. Crumble shredded wheat biscuits into meat; add sauteed onion and celery, bread crumbs, sausage, chili sauce, eggs, lemon juice, salt, Worcestershire sauce, marjoram, and pepper; toss together lightly with 2-tine fork.
6. Pack mixture into loaf pan, 9x5x3; arrange bacon slices on top.
7. Bake in moderate oven (350°F) 45 minutes.
8. Place loaf on heated platter; slice; serve with additional chili sauce, if desired.

Barbecued Calf Liver

Makes 4 servings

4 slices calf liver (about 1 pound)
¼ cup **Seasoned Flour**, page 41
2 tablespoons butter or margarine
Hot Barbecue Sauce, page 131

1. Prepare liver following directions, page 103.
2. Rub liver slices with SEASONED FLOUR.
3. Melt butter or margarine in medium-size frying pan with tight-fitting cover; brown liver quickly on both sides over medium heat; pour HOT BARBECUE SAUCE over slices; cover.
4. Simmer 10 minutes, or until flavors are well blended.
5. Place liver on heated platter; spoon sauce over each slice.

Oxtails

To Buy "Oxtails" is the trade name for the tails of all cattle. These are usually sold in 1½-inch lengths, either fresh or frozen and packaged. The proportion of bone is great and the meat is coarse-textured but its flavor is good. Buy 2 pounds for 4 servings.

To Store Store frozen oxtails in your freezer or frozen-food compartment of your refrigerator; thaw in refrigerator or cook unthawed. Store fresh oxtails, loosely wrapped, in your refrigerator. Use within 24 hours.

Sweetbreads—left to right, lamb, veal, beef

Braised Oxtails

Makes 4 servings

2 pounds oxtails, cut into 1½-inch lengths
⅓ cup **Seasoned Flour**, page 41
Melted fat to make thin film in large heavy frying pan
1 can (8 ounces) tomato sauce
1 cup water
2 tablespoons vinegar
1 medium-size onion, sliced
1 small bay leaf

1. Wash oxtail joints in cold water; dust well with SEASONED FLOUR placed in a paper bag; save remaining flour for Step 3.
2. Brown meat in hot fat in large heavy frying pan with tight-fitting cover, over medium heat; pour off any excess fat.
3. Stir in leftover flour mixture and remaining ingredients; cover tightly.
4. Bring to boiling; reduce heat; simmer 2½ to 3 hours, or until meat is tender when pierced with 2-tine fork. (Add more water during cooking, if needed.) Serve with pan gravy.

Sweetbreads

To Buy Sweetbreads are the thymus glands of calves, young steers, and lambs. There are 2 kinds, throat sweetbreads and heart sweetbreads. Both are delicate in flavor and texture, are highly prized and expensive. The pancreas (a different gland) of older beef animals is also sometimes sold as "sweetbreads" but is neither as delicate nor as delicious. Sweetbreads are sold frozen in packages or fresh. Buy 1 pound of sweetbreads for 4 servings.

To Store Keep frozen sweetbreads in your freezer or the frozen-food compartment of your refrigerator. Thaw by dropping into boiling water. Prepare fresh sweetbreads as soon as purchased (see below); keep covered in refrigerator and use within 24 hours.

To Prepare Wash sweetbreads in cold water; drop into boiling acidulated water (1 teaspoon salt and 1 table-spoon vinegar to 1 quart water); cover; *simmer* (never boil) calf or lamb sweetbreads 20 minutes, beef sweet-breads 30 minutes. Drain; plunge into cold water; hold under running cold water while slipping thin membrane off with fingers; trim out thick connec-tive tissue and fat with sharp paring knife; dry; chill.

To Cook

TO BROIL Split 2 pairs simmered sweetbreads (see preparation above) in halves lengthwise; brush with melted butter or margarine; sprinkle with salt and pepper. Broil, with top of meat 3 inches from unit or tip of flame, 5 min-utes on each side, or until golden brown, turning sweetbreads once. Sprinkle lightly with paprika; serve with MAITRE D'HOTEL BUTTER, page 130. Makes 4 servings.

TO PAN-FRY Split 2 pairs simmered sweetbreads (see preparation at left) in halves lengthwise; brush with melted butter or margarine; dip in fine bread crumbs; saute in hot butter or marga-rine until golden brown over low heat. Serve garnished with parsley and lemon quarters. Makes 4 servings.

Sweetbreads Creole

Makes 4 servings

  2 pairs sweetbreads
  ¼ cup flour
  ¼ cup salad oil
  1 small green pepper, finely chopped
  1 large onion, chopped (1 cup)
  2 cups (about 1-pound can) tomatoes
  2 teaspoons salt
1½ teaspoons sugar
  ½ teaspoon chili powder
  ½ teaspoon oregano
  ⅛ teaspoon pepper

1. Prepare sweetbreads following di-rections above; break into small pieces; dust with flour; save remaining flour for Step 4.
2. Saute sweetbreads in hot oil in large heavy frying pan over low heat until golden brown; push aside in pan.
3. Add green pepper and onion; saute over low heat 10 to 15 minutes, or just until onion is tender.
4. Stir in tomatoes, seasonings, and remaining flour.
5. Simmer 20 minutes, or until heated through. Serve with boiled rice or BROWN-BUTTER FLUFF RICE, page 135, if desired.

Sweetbreads in Wine Sauce

Bake at 375° F about 30 minutes . . . Makes 4 servings

  2 pairs sweetbreads
  2 tablespoons butter or margarine
  2 tablespoons flour
  ½ teaspoon salt
  ⅛ teaspoon pepper
  1 cup hot water
  1 beef-bouillon cube
  ½ teaspoon Worcestershire sauce
  ¼ cup dry sherry wine

1. Prepare sweetbreads following di-rections above; break into pieces; save for Step 4.
2. Melt butter or margarine in small saucepan; blend in flour, salt, and pepper; stir in water gradually; add bouillon cube; cook over low heat, stirring constantly, until sauce thick-ens and boils 1 minute.
3. Stir in Worcestershire sauce and sherry wine.
4. Place sweetbreads in 1½-quart cas-serole; cover with wine sauce.
5. Bake in moderate oven (375° F) 30 minutes.

Tongue—left to right, beef, veal, pork, lamb

Tongue

To Buy   Tongue is somewhat coarse in texture but has excellent flavor. Beef tongues are sold fresh, pickled, corned, smoked, and cooked ready-to-serve in cans, jars, or by the slice. Beef tongues weigh from 2 to 5 pounds. Veal tongues, from ½ to 2 pounds in weight, are sold fresh. Pork tongues, weighing ½ to 1¼ pounds, are usually sold as "lunch tongue" in cans or jars. Lamb tongues weigh 3 to 4 ounces each and are sold fresh, pickled, or canned. Allow 1 pound of cooked tongue for 4 servings. A 4-pound tongue makes about 8 servings when cooked.

To Store   Keep smoked tongue in original wrapper in your refrigerator. Cook within 3 days. Store fresh tongue, loosely wrapped, in refrigerator. Use within 24 hours. Pickled tongues can be kept in your refrigerator as long as a week.

To Cook   Wash thoroughly in cold water (if tongue is heavily cured, soak 2 hours in cold water to cover in order to reduce saltiness; drain). Place in Dutch oven or large kettle with tight-fitting cover; add warm water to cover, ¼ cup vinegar, 2 tablespoons brown sugar, ½ teaspoon thyme, and 8 whole cloves; cover tightly; bring to boiling; reduce heat. Simmer 2 to 4½ hours for beef tongue, 1½ hours for lamb tongue, 2 hours for pork tongue, 2½ hours for veal tongue, or until tongue is tender

when pierced with 2-tine fork. Cool in liquor 1 hour; remove; drain; pull off skin; cut off excess fat; remove small bones. Serve, sliced, hot or cold with APPLE-RAISIN SAUCE, page 132; or MUSTARD SAUCE, page 131, if desired.

Savory Smoked Tongue (Pressure Cooker)

Makes about 8 servings

    2 cups water
    ¼ cup vinegar
    2 tablespoons brown sugar
    ½ teaspoon thyme
    8 whole cloves
    1 smoked beef tongue (about 4 pounds)

1.   Combine water, vinegar, brown sugar, thyme, and cloves in 8-quart pressure cooker.
2.   Cut tongue in half crosswise; place in cooker.
3.   Cover cooker; cook at 15 pounds pressure 1 hour; cool quickly according to manufacturer's directions; remove cover.
4.   Remove tongue from cooker; cool slightly; cut away skin and excess fat; chill; slice. Or place on heated platter; serve immediately with hot APPLE-RAISIN SAUCE, page 132.

VARIATION

Smoked Tongue and Sauerkraut   Place 7 cups (2 cans: 1 pound, 13 ounces each) sauerkraut in bottom of 8-quart pressure cooker; place tongue on sauerkraut; combine 1 cup water, ½ cup vinegar, ¼ cup brown sugar (firmly packed), 6 whole cloves, and 1 bay leaf; pour over tongue and sauerkraut; cover cooker. Cook at 15 pounds pressure 1 hour; cool quickly according to manufacturer's directions; remove cover. Skin tongue; cut off excess fat; reheat tongue with sauerkraut (do not use pressure control). Makes 8 servings.

New Castle Tongue

Makes 4 servings

2 tablespoons butter or margarine
1 large onion, coarsely chopped (1 cup)
2 tablespoons flour
1 teaspoon salt
¼ teaspoon marjoram
⅛ teaspoon pepper
1 cup milk
1 package quick-frozen Fordhook lima
   beans, cooked
   Or: 1½ cups cooked lima beans
1 can (9 ounces) pineapple tidbits
2 cups diced cooked tongue

1. Melt butter or margarine in medium-size saucepan; saute onion over low heat 10 to 15 minutes, or just until tender.
2. Blend in flour, salt, marjoram, and pepper; stir in milk gradually; cook, stirring constantly, until sauce thickens and boils 1 minute.
3. Add lima beans, pineapple, and tongue; cover tightly.
4. Simmer 5 to 8 minutes, or until heated through.

Tongue and Potato Cakes

Makes 4 large cakes

1½ cups coarsely ground cooked tongue
¾ cup well-seasoned mashed potatoes
   Butter or margarine for browning
   cakes

1. Combine tongue and mashed potatoes in medium-size bowl; blend.
2. Shape into 4 cakes.
3. Melt butter or margarine in medium-size frying pan; brown cakes on both sides over medium heat until crust is golden and crisp.

Tongue Croquettes Substitute 2 cups ground cooked tongue in recipe for HAM CROQUETTES, page 93.

Variety Meats Menus

Savory Smoked Tongue*
Hot Apple-Raisin Sauce*
Macaroni Salad
Poppy-Seed Rolls   Butter
Chilled Cantaloupe
Beverage

* *

Savory Liver and Sausage Bake*
Mashed Potatoes   Coleslaw
Oven-Toasted Rolls
Hot Gingerbread
Canned Peaches
Beverage

* *

Sweetbreads Creole*
Rice   Green Beans
Mixed Fruit Salad
Rolls   Butter
Chocolate Cake
Beverage

* *

Shrimp Cocktail
Broiled Kidneys, Marinade*
Green Beans
Mashed Potatoes
Lettuce Wedges   French Dressing
Hawaiian Fruit Cup
Beverage

* *

Braised Oxtails*
Buttered Noodles   Coleslaw
Crusty Rolls   Butter
Apple Pie
Beverage

*For recipes see index

Quick-Fix Meats

You will find a whole array of easy-to-prepare-and-serve meats in your grocery market. Try zesty sausages (cold cuts); frankfurters; sliced precooked tongue, ham, or roast beef; or one of the many canned meats next time you have a busy day.

Sausages

To Buy *Sausages,* or *cold cuts,* have been favorite meats since Greek and Roman times. They are prepared from varying combinations of minced meats mixed with many different herbs, spices, and condiments. Sausage making began in the hot Mediterranean countries as a means of preserving meat. The dry, hard types were made first. Later, the softer, milder sausages were developed in northern European countries.

There are more than 200 varieties made and sold in the United States today. These are divided into 4 groups:

1. *Uncooked fresh sausage* such as pork sausage links, bockwurst, and fresh thuringer-style sausage.
Uncooked smoked sausage such as Polish-style and country-style pork sausage.
2. *Cooked plain* or *smoked sausage,* such as frankfurters, bologna (big and little), knockwurst, Vienna sausages, and the liver sausages (Braunschweiger, liver and bacon, Strassburg, liver cheese). These are ready to eat but may have additional cooking.
3. *Dry* or *semi-dry sausage* such as the salamis (Genoa, Milan, cooked, hard), blockwurst, capocollo, pork roll, pepperoni, cervelat, and· thuringer. These are highly seasoned, ready-to-eat meats, often called *summer sausages.*

4. *Cooked specialties* such as veal loaf, pickle-and-pimiento loaf, blood tongue loaf, four-in-one loaf, old-fashioned loaf, special loaf, kubama loaf, luxury loaf, macaroni-and-cheese loaf, olive-and-pimiento loaf, pickle-pimiento loaf, and the gelatin specialties such as souse, headcheese, and jellied corned beef.

Sausages are put up in 3 types of casings — natural, cloth, and artificial transparent. The natural casings are edible, others must be removed before serving.

These meats are thrifty, because there is no waste. Buy 1 pound uncooked sausage, ⅓ to ½ pound dry or semi-dry sausage, or ¾ to 1 pound cooked specialties for 4 servings. For cold meat platters buy 3 or more kinds, allowing about 3 ounces of meat per ·serving.

To Store Keep in original wrappings or wrap in waxed paper or aluminum foil; store *flat* in your refrigerator. If bought in the piece, do not slice until you are ready to use it. Use sliced cold cuts within 2 or 3 days. Many of these will keep up to 2 weeks in your refrigerator, but they are best when fresh.

Quick Sausage Casserole

Bake at 350°F about 40 minutes . . .
Makes 4 servings

½ pound Polish-style sausage, cut into
    bite-size pieces
1 can condensed cream of mushroom
    soup
1 cup milk or water
1 pimiento, diced
½ cup diced green pepper.
4 ounces (half an 8-ounce package)
    noodles

1. Combine sausage, soup, milk or water, pimiento, green pepper, and noodles in 1½-quart casserole; cover.
2. Bake in moderate oven (350°F) 40 minutes, or until noodles and pepper are tender.

Pepperoni and Macaroni au Gratin

Bake at 375°F about 30 minutes . . .
Makes 4 servings

    2 cups **Cheese Sauce**, page 128, made
      with **Thin White Sauce**
    2 cups (half an 8-ounce package)
      drained cooked macaroni
    ⅓ pound pepperoni, diced
    4 green apples, pared, cored, and
      thinly sliced

1. Combine hot CHEESE SAUCE, macaroni, pepperoni, and apple in well-greased 1½-quart casserole; mix thoroughly.
2. Bake in moderate oven (375°F) 30 minutes, or until apple is tender and top is evenly browned.

Sausage Blintzes

Makes 4 servings

    2 eggs
1 ½ cups milk
    1 cup sifted flour
    ½ teaspoon salt
    8 slices liver sausage

1. Beat eggs slightly in medium-size bowl; stir in milk.
2. Measure flour and salt into sifter; sift into egg-milk mixture; beat with rotary beater until batter is smooth. Be light-handed as over-beating batter tends to toughen pancakes. Batter will be thin.
3. Ladle about ¼ cup batter at a time onto heated greaseless griddle or into lightly greased hot heavy frying pan to form pancake.

4. Bake until top appears dry; turn; bake on other side.
5. Place 1 slice liver sausage* on each blintz; roll up; place on heated platter; keep hot until all blintzes are made.
6. Serve with sour cream.

VARIATION

Zesty Sausage Blintzes Spread each slice of liver sausage with prepared mustard or India relish before rolling.

Cold-Meat Platter Suggestions

Serve colorful platters of cold cuts at your next buffet luncheon or big get-together, or to give the family supper a lift. Choose several kinds with an eye for colors, shapes, textures, and flavors. Garnish with sliced cheeses, olives, tomato wedges, sprigs of water cress or parsley, pickles, fruits, or relishes. Arrange the meats to make serving easy.

Cold-Platter Combinations:
1. Smoked salami, liver sausage, luxury loaf, and knockwurst.
2. Bologna, Genoa salami, spiced ham loaf, and pepperoni.
3. Pickle-pimiento loaf, Braunschweiger, cooked salami, and capocollo.
4. Cervelat, bologna, and spiced luncheon meat.
5. Blood-and-tongue bologna, head-cheese, hard salami, and ham-and-cheese loaf.
6. Liver sausage, pimiento loaf, and cooked thuringer sausage.
7. Spiced ham, liverwurst, pepperoni, and knockwurst.
8. Meat loaf, smoked salami, cervelat, and bologna.

It is easier to keep blintzes hot if liver sausage is warm when rolled into pancake. Heat in double boiler, if desired.

Pepperoni Pilaf

Makes 4 servings

2 tablespoons butter or margarine
1 medium-size onion, chopped (½ cup)
½ pound pepperoni, diced
1 cup raw rice
1 can (3 or 4 ounces) sliced mushrooms
2 cups (about 1-pound can) tomatoes
½ cup diced celery
½ bay leaf
1½ cups water

1. Melt butter or margarine in 4-quart saucepan with tight-fitting cover; saute onion over low heat 5 minutes, or just until tender.
2. Add pepperoni; saute 1 to 2 minutes; stir in rice, mushrooms, tomatoes, celery, bay leaf, and water; cover.
3. Bring to boiling; reduce heat; simmer 50 to 60 minutes, or until rice is tender and liquid is absorbed.

Salami Patties

Makes 4 servings

1 egg, slightly beaten
¼ pound salami, ground
1 cup cooked rice (about ¼ cup raw)
   Or: 1 cup riced cooked potatoes (about 1 medium-size)
2 teaspoons chopped parsley
¼ teaspoon marjoram
1 tablespoon melted butter or margarine
¼ cup milk
½ cup fine dry bread crumbs
2 tablespoons fat

1. Combine egg, salami, rice or potatoes, parsley, marjoram, and butter or margarine in medium-size bowl; toss together lightly with 2-tine fork.
2. Shape into 8 patties; dip in milk; coat with bread crumbs; chill.
3. Brown patties on both sides over medium heat in hot fat in large heavy frying pan.

4. Serve with APPLE-RAISIN SAUCE, page 132, or MUSTARD SAUCE, page 131, if desired.

VARIATION
Bologna Patties Substitute 1 cup ground bologna for salami; add ¼ teaspoon salt and ⅛ teaspoon pepper to other ingredients in Step 1 at left.

Salami and Eggs

Makes 4 servings

1 tablespoon butter or margarine
¼ cup diced celery
¼ pound salami or Polish-style sausage, sliced
4 eggs, unbeaten
¼ cup milk
Salt and pepper
Paprika

1. Melt butter or margarine in medium-size frying pan; saute celery over low heat 10 minutes, or just until tender.
2. Remove casing from sausage; fry slices in same pan on each side 2 minutes, or just until hot.
3. Beat eggs slightly in medium-size bowl; stir in milk, salt and pepper to taste, and paprika.
4. Pour egg mixture into pan with celery and sausage.
5. Cook, stirring constantly, until eggs are cooked the way you like them.
6. Serve piping hot with TOMATO SAUCE, page 130, if desired.

Right—A lazy-susan supper: Liver sausage and fluted cucumber slices; ripe and stuffed green olives; green onions wrapped in slices of pickle-pimiento loaf; stuffed eggs; BOLOGNA-CHEESE TRIANGLES; tomato wedges; sticks of process American cheese wrapped in salami slices; water cress and carrot curls; spiced ham and thin slices of raw cauliflower—all arranged around a salad.

Salami-Rice Loaf

Bake at 325°F about 50 minutes . . .
Makes 6 servings

¼ pound sliced salami
2 cups cooked rice (about ½ cup raw)
½ cup fine dry bread crumbs
¼ cup chopped celery
2 tablespoons chopped parsley
2 tablespoons finely chopped onion
2 eggs, slightly beaten
1 can condensed cream of mushroom soup
Mustard Sauce, page 131

1. Grease loaf pan, 9x5x3; line bottom with waxed paper; grease paper.
2. Cut 6 strips from middle of salami slices; place strips crosswise in bottom of prepared loaf pan.
3. Chop remaining salami fine; place in medium-size bowl.
4. Add remaining ingredients; toss with fork until blended.
5. Pack into loaf pan; place in pan of hot water (water should be 1 inch deep).
6. Bake in slow oven (325° F) 50 minutes, or until loaf is set in center.
7. Remove loaf pan from hot water at once; cool slightly.
8. Loosen around edges with knife or spatula; turn out onto heated platter; remove waxed paper.
9. Serve with MUSTARD SAUCE.

Diana's Sausage Surprise

Bake at 350°F about 1 hour . . .
Makes 4 servings

2 eggs, unbeaten
1½ cups milk
1 cup sifted flour
½ teaspoon salt
½ pound uncooked hot Italian sausage

1. Beat eggs slightly in medium-size bowl; stir in milk.

2. Measure flour and salt into sifter; sift into egg-milk mixture; beat with rotary beater until batter is smooth; chill 30 minutes.
3. Remove skin from sausage; divide into 20 equal portions; shape into small balls (sausage is highly seasoned, so keep them small); brown balls well over low heat in medium-size frying pan.
4. Place balls and 2 tablespoons hot sausage fat in 2-quart casserole; pour chilled batter over meat.
5. Bake in moderate oven (350°F) 1 hour, or until batter has risen and is evenly browned and crisp.

Cervelat-Stuffed Green Peppers

Bake at 375°F about 30 minutes . . .
Makes 4 servings

4 medium-size green peppers
1 tablespoon butter or margarine
1 medium-size onion, chopped (½ cup)
¼ pound cervelat, finely diced
1½ cups cooked rice
¼ cup tomato sauce
½ teaspoon salt
⅛ teaspoon pepper
⅛ teaspoon marjoram

1. Cut ½-inch slice from stem end of each green pepper; save ends; remove all seeds and membranes from peppers; cook shells and ends in large amount boiling salted water in large kettle 5 minutes; drain; save for Step 3.
2. Melt butter or margarine in medium-size saucepan; saute onion over low heat 5 minutes, or just until tender; stir in cervelat, rice, tomato sauce, salt, pepper, and marjoram.
3. Fill peppers with stuffing; cover with stem ends.
4. Place peppers upright in shallow baking dish; pour boiling water around peppers to depth of ½ inch.

5. Bake in moderate oven (375° F) 30 minutes, or until peppers are tender. Serve with TOMATO SAUCE, page 130.

Sausage Ring

Bake at 375° F for 20 to 25 minutes...
Makes 4 to 6 servings

½ pound thuringer sausage
1 large onion, quartered
2 stalks of celery
2 tablespoons chopped parsley
2 tablespoons grated Parmesan cheese
¼ teaspoon paprika
⅛ teaspoon pepper
1½ cups biscuit mix
½ cup milk
2 tablespoons melted butter or margarine

1. Put sausage, onion, and celery through chopper, using coarse perforated plate; combine with parsley, cheese, paprika, and pepper in medium-size bowl; save for Step 4.
2. Prepare biscuit according to directions on package of mix, using ½ cup milk.
3. Turn dough out onto lightly floured pastry cloth or board; knead 1 minute, adding a little more flour, if needed, to keep dough from sticking; roll into rectangle, 12x14.
4. Spread sausage-onion filling evenly over dough to within ¼ inch of edge.
5. Starting at one long edge, roll up dough, jelly-roll fashion.
6. Place roll, seam side down, on well greased cooky sheet; shape to form a ring; join ends by pinching together.
7. Mark top of roll into 12 even sections; cut almost to center with scissors or sharp knife, leaving about ½ inch of uncut dough at inside edge of ring.
8. Twist cut sections, one at a time, overlapping each in same direction, so part of cut edge rests on cooky sheet, part on twisted section before it.

To form SAUSAGE RING, twist cut sections, overlapping each in the same direction.

9. Brush ring with melted butter or margarine.
10. Bake in moderate oven (375° F) 20 to 25 minutes, or until golden brown. Serve with HORSERADISH SAUCE, page 128, if desired.

Creamed Knockwurst and Potatoes

Makes 4 servings

2 tablespoons butter or margarine
1 large onion, coarsely chopped (1 cup)
2 tablespoons flour
1 teaspoon salt
⅛ teaspoon pepper
2 cups milk
¾ pound knockwurst, cut into ½-inch cubes
4 cups diced peeled cooked potatoes (about 5 medium-size)
2 tablespoons chopped parsley

1. Melt butter or margarine in medium-size saucepan with tight-fitting cover; saute onion over low heat 10 to 15 minutes, or until tender.
2. Blend in flour, salt, and pepper; slowly stir in milk.
3. Cook, stirring constantly, until mixture thickens and boils 1 minute.
4. Add sausage, potatoes, and parsley; cover tightly.
5. Cook 5 to 10 minutes, or just until mixture is heated through.

BARBECUED BOLOGNA ROLL

Finger-Food Roll-Ups

Spoon well-seasoned cottage cheese down the middle of large thin slices of bologna. Roll up into easy-to-eat cylinders; fasten each with a wooden pick.

Jiffy Bake

Bake at 375°F about 20 minutes . . .
Makes 4 servings

> 2 cans (about 1 pound each) cooked macaroni with cheese sauce
> ½ pound sliced bologna

1.   Empty 1 can macaroni and cheese into greased 1-quart baking dish.
2.   Quarter bologna slices; arrange half of quartered slices in layer on macaroni and cheese.
3.   Top bologna layer with contents of second can macaroni and cheese; arrange remaining bologna quarters in circle design on top; cover tightly.
4.   Bake in moderate oven (375°F) 20 minutes, or until bubbly and hot.

Bologna-Cheese Triangles

Makes 8 triangles

> 2 packages (3 ounces each) cream cheese
> 1 tablespoon evaporated milk or cream
> ½ teaspoon minced onion
> ½ teaspoon prepared mustard
> ⅛ teaspoon salt
> 8 slices (about ½ pound) big bologna

1.   Blend cream cheese, milk or cream, onion, mustard, and salt until smooth in small bowl.
2.   Spread cheese mixture between slices of bologna to make 2 four-decker sandwiches; wrap in waxed paper; chill until cheese is firm.
3.   Cut into quarters just before serving. Serve cold as an appetizer or as part of a cold-meat platter. See photograph, page 111.

Barbecued Bologna Roll

Bake at 350°F about 40 minutes . . .
Makes 4 to 6 servings

> 2 cans (8 ounces each) tomato sauce
> 1 cup water
> 1 medium-size onion, chopped (½ cup)
> 1 teaspoon chili powder
> 1 teaspoon dry mustard
> 1 teaspoon sugar
> 1 teaspoon salt
> 1 teaspoon paprika
> ¼ teaspoon pepper
> 1 pound unsliced big bologna
> 1 large mild onion, thinly sliced

1.   Combine all ingredients except bologna and onion slices in medium-size saucepan; bring to boiling; reduce heat; simmer, stirring occasionally, 30 minutes, or until flavors are blended.
2.   Make evenly spaced crosswise cuts almost through bologna with sharp knife; tuck a thin slice of mild onion in each cut; place roll in baking pan.
3.   Pour sauce over roll.
4.   Bake in moderate oven (350°F) 40 minutes, or until meat is heated through, basting often with sauce during cooking.
5.   Place roll on heated platter; pour sauce from baking pan into a bowl to pass at the table.

Frankfurters

Frankfurters are the most versatile and best-loved of the sausages. They are made of beef, pork, and sometimes veal combined with spices and seasonings. The meat is ground and stuffed into tender casings and smoked. Skinless frankfurters are made by removing casings after smoking. Most high-grade frankfurters contain 60% lean beef and 40% fat pork.

Wieners and Vienna sausages are similar to frankfurters in taste. Wieners are longer and smaller in diameter. Vienna sausages are smaller in size and are usually sold canned.

To Buy Frankfurters, whether skinless or in natural casing, come in three styles—all-meat, all-beef, and Kosher. Some frankfurters contain cereals as filler. They are sold in ½- and 1-pound cellophane-wrapped packages, in 2- or 3-pound cartons, and in cans and jars. Regular-size frankfurters average 8 to 10 to the pound; dinner frankfurters, 5 to the pound; and cocktail frankfurters, 26 to 28 per pound. Buy 1 to 2 regular-size frankfurters per serving.

To Store Keep in coldest part of your refrigerator in original wrappings, or wrap loosely in waxed paper or aluminum foil. Use within 4 days. Frankfurters may be frozen and held about 1 month in your freezer if wrapped in moisture-proof freezer wrapping material.

To Heat

TO SIMMER Drop frankfurters into kettle of boiling water; cover; reduce heat; *simmer* 5 to 8 minutes; lift out with tongs so as not to pierce the skin.
TO PAN-BROIL Brown over medium heat in small amount hot fat in heavy frying pan. Turn with tongs.
TO BROIL Brush with melted butter or margarine; broil, with top of meat 3 inches from unit or tip of flame, about 5 minutes on each side.

Broiled Stuffed Frankfurters

Makes 6 servings

> 1 can (about 1 pound) baked beans
> 1 tablespoon prepared mustard
> 2 tablespoons finely chopped onion
> 2 tablespoons vinegar
> 6 frankfurters (about ¾ pound)

1. Combine baked beans, mustard, onion, and vinegar in medium-size pan; heat through.
2. Split frankfurters almost through lengthwise; place in shallow baking pan; stuff with bean mixture.
3. Broil, with tops of frankfurters 3 inches from unit or tip of flame, 5 to 6 minutes, or until frankfurters are hot.

Skillet Franks with Barbecue Sauce

Makes 4 servings

> 1 small onion, chopped (¼ cup)
> 2 tablespoons chopped green pepper
> 2 tablespoons fat
> ¾ cup canned pineapple juice
> ½ cup catsup
> ⅛ teaspoon chili powder
> 8 frankfurters (about 1 pound)

1. Saute onion and green pepper in hot fat in large heavy frying pan over low heat 10 minutes, or just until onion is tender.
2. Stir in pineapple juice, catsup, and chili powder; bring to boiling; reduce heat; simmer 10 minutes.
3. Score frankfurters with sharp knife; place in frying pan with sauce.
4. Simmer 5 minutes, or until frankfurters are heated through.

Susan's Poncho Pups

Bake at 500°F for 8 to 10 minutes...
Makes 8 servings

8 frankfurter rolls
½ cup (from an 8-ounce jar) soft process cheese spread
8 frankfurters (about 1 pound)
4 teaspoons prepared mustard
8 slices bacon

1. Split rolls almost through; spread cheese on cut surfaces.
2. Split frankfurters almost through lengthwise; spread cut surfaces with prepared mustard; tuck into prepared rolls.
3. Cut bacon slices in half crosswise; lay 2 halves diagonally across top of each roll.
4. Place prepared frankfurters on rack in large shallow pan.
5. Bake in very hot oven (500°F) 8 to 10 minutes, or until bacon is crisp and frankfurters are heated through.

Rice, Cheese, and Frankfurter Casserole

Bake at 350°F about 45 minutes...
Makes 6 servings

2 cups cooked rice (about ½ cup raw)
3 eggs, slightly beaten
1½ cups milk
1 teaspoon salt
2 teaspoons prepared mustard
1 teaspoon Worcestershire sauce
6 frankfurters (about ¾ pound)
¼ pound process American cheese, cut into thin strips

1. Spread rice evenly over bottom of greased baking dish, 10x6x2.
2. Blend eggs, milk, and seasonings in small bowl; pour over rice; stir with fork to blend.
3. Split frankfurters lengthwise almost through; stuff with cheese strips; arrange on top of rice.

4. Place baking dish in pan of hot water (water should be 1 inch deep).
5. Bake in moderate oven (350°F) 45 minutes, or until custard is set.

Fluffy Potato and Frankfurter Casserole

Bake at 375°F about 20 minutes...
Makes 6 servings

6 tablespoons butter or margarine
1 medium-size onion, chopped (½ cup)
½ cup milk
1 teaspoon salt
¼ teaspoon paprika
⅛ teaspoon pepper
5 cups hot unseasoned mashed potatoes (about 6 medium-size)
6 frankfurters (about ¾ pound)
2 tablespoons prepared mustard
½ pound process American cheese
½ cup evaporated milk or cream

1. Melt 2 tablespoons butter or margarine in small frying pan; saute onion over low heat 5 minutes, or just until tender.
2. Beat onion, remaining 4 tablespoons butter or margarine, milk, salt, paprika, and pepper into mashed potatoes; spoon into greased baking dish, 12x7x2; spread evenly.
3. Split frankfurters through lengthwise; spread cut surfaces with prepared mustard; arrange down middle of potatoes, cut side up.
4. Bake in moderate oven (375°F) 20 minutes, or until frankfurters and potatoes are piping hot.
5. Slice cheese into top of double boiler; heat over simmering water until cheese melts while potato-frankfurter mixture bakes.
6. Blend in evaporated milk or cream slowly; cook, stirring constantly, until sauce is smooth.
7. Serve cheese sauce to spoon over potatoes and frankfurters.

Corn-Bread Shortcake

Makes 4 to 6 servings

  1 package corn-muffin mix
  ¼ cup (½ stick) butter or margarine
  ¼ cup flour
  1 small onion, finely chopped (¼ cup)
  2 tablespoons prepared mustard
  ¾ teaspoon salt
  2 cups milk
  6 frankfurters (about ¾ pound), cut
    into ¼-inch rings

1. Prepare corn bread according to directions on package of mix; bake in pan, 8x8x2.
2. Melt butter or margarine in medium-size saucepan.
3. Blend in flour, onion, mustard, and salt; slowly stir in milk.
4. Cook over low heat, stirring constantly, until sauce thickens and boils 1 minute.
5. Stir frankfurter rings into sauce; keep hot.
6. Cut baked corn bread into servings; split each piece horizontally; place bottom halves on heated platter; spoon over half the creamed frankfurters; cover with remaining corn bread; spoon rest of creamed frankfurters over tops.

Hot-Dog Roll-Ups

Bake at 450°F for 10 to 15 minutes...
Makes 4 servings, 2 roll-ups each

  2 cups biscuit mix
  ½ cup milk
  ¼ cup prepared hot-dog relish
  8 frankfurters (about 1 pound)
  ½ cup chili sauce

1. Combine biscuit mix and milk in medium-size bowl; stir to make soft dough.
2. Turn out onto lightly floured pastry cloth or board; knead lightly about ½ minute, adding a little more flour, if needed, to keep dough from sticking.
3. Roll dough to rectangle, 16x8; cut in half lengthwise; cut halves 3 times crosswise to make 8 squares, 4x4.
4. Spread about 1½ teaspoons hot-dog relish down middle of each square; place a frankfurter on top; wrap dough around it, sealing seam by pinching edges together; place, seam side down, on ungreased cooky sheet.
5. Bake in hot oven (450°F) 10 to 15 minutes, or until biscuit rolls are golden brown.
6. Heat chili sauce in small saucepan; serve over hot roll-ups.

VARIATION

Mustard Roll-Ups Spread prepared mustard over each square of dough instead of hot-dog relish before rolling.

Frankfurters in Mustard Sauce

Makes 6 servings

  ¼ cup (½ stick) butter or margarine
  6 frankfurters (about ¾ pound), cut in
    ½-inch rings
  1 small onion, sliced
  ¼ cup flour
  2 teaspoons prepared mustard
  ½ teaspoon salt
    Dash of pepper
  1 cup evaporated milk
  1 cup fresh milk
  6 slices toast, buttered

1. Melt butter or margarine in large heavy frying pan; saute frankfurters and onion over low heat 5 minutes, or just until onion is tender.
2. Blend in flour, mustard, salt, and pepper; gradually stir in evaporated and fresh milks.
3. Cook, stirring constantly, until mixture thickens and boils 1 minute. Serve on buttered toast.

Elizabeth's Bake

Bake at 400°F about 35 minutes . . .
Makes 4 servings

3½ cups (1-pound, 13-ounce can)
    sauerkraut, drained
  1 cup dried prunes, pitted and cut into
    small pieces
  1 small onion, chopped (¼ cup)
  1 tablespoon sugar
  ½ teaspoon salt
  ½ cup apple juice
  3 cups hot seasoned mashed potatoes
    (about 4 medium-size)
  8 frankfurters (about 1 pound)

1. Combine sauerkraut, prunes, onion, sugar, salt, and apple juice in baking dish, 12x7x2; toss together lightly with 2-tine fork; spread evenly; cover with aluminum foil.
2. Bake in moderately hot oven (400°F) 15 minutes; remove from oven; leave heat on.
3. Spoon mashed potatoes on sauerkraut to make a border around edge; score frankfurters with sharp knife; place on sauerkraut in center of baking dish; return to oven.
4. Bake 20 minutes, or until potatoes are browned and frankfurters hot.

Pine Valley Red Hots

Makes 6 servings

  2 tablespoons butter or margarine
  1 large onion, chopped (1 cup)
  ½ cup chopped celery
  2 cans (8 ounces each) tomato sauce
  2 tablespoons brown sugar
  2 tablespoons lemon juice
  1 tablespoon Worcestershire sauce
  1 teaspoon chili powder
  ½ teaspoon salt
  ½ teaspoon prepared mustard
  12 frankfurters (about 1½ pounds)

1. Melt butter or margarine in large heavy frying pan with tight-fitting cover; saute onion and celery over low heat 10 to 15 minutes, or just until onion is tender.
2. Stir in tomato sauce, brown sugar, lemon juice, Worcestershire sauce, chili powder, salt, and mustard; cover tightly.
3. Bring to boiling; reduce heat; simmer 20 minutes to blend flavors.
4. Add frankfurters; cover; simmer 15 minutes to heat through, basting once or twice during cooking.
5. Place frankfurters on heated platter; spoon sauce over; sprinkle extra chopped onion and celery over top, if desired. See photograph at right.

Sweet and Pungent Frankfurters

Makes 4 generous servings

  4 frankfurters (about ½ pound), cut into
    ½-inch rings
  1 can (about 1 pound) meatless chop
    suey
  1 can (9 ounces) pineapple tidbits
  1 large green pepper, diced
  1 medium-size onion, chopped (½ cup)
  ⅓ cup vinegar
  2 tablespoons sugar
  2 tablespoons soy sauce
  1 can (3¾ ounces) fried noodles

1. Combine frankfurters, chop suey, pineapple and juice, green pepper, onion, vinegar, sugar, and soy sauce in medium-size saucepan with tight-fitting cover; cover tightly.
2. Bring to boiling; reduce heat; simmer 15 minutes to blend flavors. (Pepper and onion will be tender-crisp.)
3. Heat noodles according to directions on can while frankfurters simmer.
4. Serve frankfurter mixture over noodles on heated plates.

Right—PINE VALLEY RED HOTS

Simple Simon Bean Bake

Bake at 375°F about 20 minutes . . .
Makes 4 servings

 2 cans (about 1 pound each) baked
    beans
 ½ cup catsup
 1 small onion, finely chopped (¼ cup)
 1 tablespoon brown sugar
 4 frankfurters (about ½ pound), split
    almost through lengthwise
 ½ cup grated process American cheese

1. Combine beans, catsup, onion, and
brown sugar in baking dish, 10x6x2.
2. Arrange frankfurters on top;
sprinkle with cheese.
3. Bake in moderate oven (375°F) 20
minutes, or until bubbly hot.

15-Minute Frankfurters 'n' Noodles

Makes 4 servings

 ¼ cup (½ stick) butter or margarine
 1 medium-size onion, chopped (½ cup)
2¼ cups (1-pint, 2-ounce can) tomato
    juice
1¼ cups water
 1 teaspoon sugar
 1 teaspoon dry mustard
 1 teaspoon meat-extract paste
 ½ teaspoon salt
 4 ounces (half an 8-ounce package)
    wide noodles
 8 frankfurters (about 1 pound), cut into
    ¼-inch rings

1. Melt butter or margarine in large
heavy frying pan with tight-fitting
cover; saute onion over low heat 5 minutes, or just until tender.
2. Stir in remaining ingredients;
cover tightly.
3. Bring to boiling; reduce heat; simmer until noodles are tender, stirring
mixture often to keep noodles from
sticking.

Canned Meats

Canned meats are so easy to buy, store,
and use that they are a popular staple
food. There are more than 25 different
kinds to choose from, packed in sizes
from individual servings to enough for
50 servings. Included are:

Canned meats such as corned beef,
roast beef, dried beef, pork luncheon
meat, hamburgers, ham loaf, ham,
meat balls, meat loaf, roast mutton,
pigs' feet, pork, corned pork, sausage,
scrapple, tongue, tripe, veal loaf, and
roast veal.

Meat combinations or *specialties* such
as beef à la mode, beef and gravy, beef
and noodles, beef and onions, beef
stew, chile con carne, chili con carne
without beans, chop suey, corned beef
hash, frankfurters with sauerkraut,
frankfurters with sauce, beef goulash,
ravioli, pork and sauerkraut, pork and
gravy, spaghetti and meat balls, steak
and gravy, kidney stew, lamb stew,
tamales, and veal and noodles.

Meat spreads (packed in 2¼- to 4½-
ounce cans) such as deviled ham, liver
spread, tongue spread, and corned-
beef spread.

 Use canned meats cold in appetizers,
salads, sandwiches, and on cold platters. Use them hot in casseroles, sauces,
or in combinations with rice, macaroni, potatoes, or spaghetti.

To Buy Seasonings vary somewhat, so
buy the brand you like. Quantities generally make from 2 to 4 servings.

To Store Canned meats can be purchased in quantity and stored at room
temperature unless the labels state
otherwise (as in the case of large hams
that must be kept in the refrigerator
and used within a short time). When
opened, however, the contents should
be used within 2 or 3 days.

Chili Casserole

Bake at 350°F for 25 to 30 minutes...
Makes 6 servings

1 cup (half a 4-ounce package) corn chips, coarsely crushed
1 can (about 1 pound) chili con carne with beans
1 can condensed tomato soup
1 medium-size onion, chopped (½ cup)

1. Cover bottom of greased 1-quart baking dish with half the corn chips.
2. Combine chili con carne, soup, and onion in medium-size bowl; pour over corn chips in baking dish.
3. Top mixture with remaining corn chips.
4. Bake in moderate oven (350°F) 25 to 30 minutes, or until piping hot.

Jiffy Chili Con Carne

Makes 6 to 8 servings

2½ cups **Savory Meat Sauce**, page 21
2 cans (about 1 pound each) baked red kidney beans
2 teaspoons chili powder
¼ teaspoon salt

1. Combine ingredients in large saucepan; simmer 20 minutes to blend flavors.
2. Serve hot over buttered toast, if desired.

Quick Chili Spaghetti

Bake at 350°F about 20 minutes...
Makes 4 servings

1 package (8 ounces) thin spaghetti
1 can (about 1 pound) chili con carne without beans
1 can condensed tomato soup
½ can water (measured in soup can)
1 small onion, finely chopped (¼ cup)
Grated Parmesan cheese

CHILI CASSEROLE

1. Cook spaghetti according to directions on package in medium-size saucepan; drain; return to same pan.
2. Stir in chili con carne, tomato soup, water, and onion; spoon into 2-quart baking dish; sprinkle generously with cheese.
3. Bake in moderate oven (350°F) 20 minutes, or until bubbly hot and lightly browned on top.

Quick Croquettes

Bake at 450°F about 15 minutes...
Makes 4 servings

Combine ½ cup mayonnaise or salad dressing; 1 can (12 ounces) pork luncheon meat, ground; and 2 cups (about 4 slices) soft bread crumbs; shape into 4 croquettes; roll in ¼ cup fine dry bread crumbs. Bake in hot oven (450°F) 15 minutes, or until croquettes are lightly browned.

Ham 'n' Cheese Savories

Blend 1 can deviled ham and ⅓ cup grated process American cheese. Open and separate 1 package refrigerated ready-to-bake biscuits; place on baking sheet; spread ham mixture over tops of biscuits. Bake in hot oven (450°F) 8 to 10 minutes, or until biscuits are brown and bubbly on top. Serve hot.

121

Luncheon Bean Bake

Bake at 375°F about 40 minutes...
Makes 4 servings

> 2 cans (about 1 pound each) baked
> beans
> 1 medium-size onion, chopped (½ cup)
> 1½ tablespoons vinegar
> 2 tablespoons brown sugar
> ¼ teaspoon dry mustard
> 1 can (12 ounces) pork luncheon meat
> 1 can (9 ounces) pineapple slices,
> drained

1. Spread beans in shallow 1-quart baking dish; stir in onion and vinegar; sprinkle brown sugar and mustard over top.
2. Make 6 crosswise cuts in meat almost through loaf; halve 3 pineapple slices (use remaining slice for fruit cup); tuck 1 piece in each cut in meat to form a fan-shape loaf.
3. Place meat fan on top of beans in baking dish; brush top with pineapple juice from can; cover tightly.
4. Bake in moderate oven (375°F) 40 minutes, or until beans and meat are heated through. Uncover during last 15 minutes to brown meat.

Orange Ham Loaf

Bake at 375°F about 20 minutes...
Makes 4 servings

> 1 can (12 ounces) pork luncheon meat
> 2 large oranges, peeled and sectioned
> ½ cup brown sugar, firmly packed
> 1 tablespoon flour
> 1 teaspoon dry mustard
> ½ cup water
> 1 teaspoon grated lemon rind
> 1½ tablespoons lemon juice
> 1½ tablespoons vinegar
> ⅓ cup seedless raisins

1. Make 6 crosswise cuts in meat almost through loaf; tuck orange sections in each cut in meat to form a fan-shape loaf.

2. Place meat fan in shallow baking pan.
3. Combine remaining ingredients in small saucepan.
4. Cook over low heat, stirring constantly, until sauce thickens and boils 1 minute.
5. Spoon sauce over loaf.
6. Bake in moderate oven (375°F) 20 minutes, or until meat and oranges are hot and glazed, basting often during baking.
7. Place on heated platter; spoon sauce over loaf.

Chevron Rice Bake

Bake at 325°F about 45 minutes...
Makes 6 servings

> 4 cups cooked rice (about 1 cup raw)
> 1 can (about 1 pound) peas, drained
> 2 eggs, slightly beaten
> 1 can condensed cream of chicken soup
> ½ cup milk
> ¼ cup (½ stick) melted butter or
> margarine
> ¼ cup chopped parsley
> 1 small onion, finely chopped (¼ cup)
> ¾ teaspoon curry powder
> ½ teaspoon salt
> ⅛ teaspoon pepper
> 1 can (12 ounces) pork luncheon meat
> 6 canned peach halves, drained
> 12 whole cloves

1. Combine rice, peas, eggs, soup, milk, butter or margarine, parsley, onion, curry powder, salt, and pepper in large bowl.
2. Slice ¼ of the meat into 10 to 12 strips about ¼ inch thick; save for topping. Dice remaining meat; stir into rice mixture; toss together lightly with 2-tine fork.
3. Spoon into well-greased 2-quart casserole; spread evenly.
4. Stud each peach half with 2 whole cloves; place peaches in row down middle of rice-meat mixture; arrange

CHEVRON RICE BAKE

meat strips on each side of peaches to make chevron design. See photograph, above.

5. Bake in slow oven (325°F) 45 minutes, or until heated through and meat on top is lightly browned.

Fried Rice Ring with Savory Meat Sauce

Makes 4 servings

Rice Ring

4 cups cooked rice (about 1 cup raw)
1 medium-size onion, finely chopped (½ cup)
2 tablespoons salad oil
2 tablespoons soy sauce

Sauce

¼ cup (½ stick) butter or margarine
1 small onion, finely chopped (¼ cup)
¼ cup flour
1 teaspoon prepared mustard
¼ teaspoon salt
2 cups milk
1 can (12 ounces) pork luncheon meat, finely diced

1. Combine rice, onion, salad oil, and soy sauce in large heavy frying pan.
2. Fry over low heat, stirring often with 2-tine fork, 10 minutes, or until rice is golden; keep hot.
3. MAKE SAUCE: Melt butter or margarine in medium-size saucepan over low heat; saute onion 5 minutes, or just until tender; blend in flour, mustard, and salt; slowly stir in milk.
4. Cook, stirring constantly, until sauce thickens and boils 1 minute.
5. Add diced meat; heat just to boiling.
6. Spoon hot rice in ring on heated platter; fill center with meat sauce.

Luncheon Surprise

Makes 8 to 12 servings

3 cans (12 ounces each) pork luncheon meat, finely chopped
1 cup sweet pickle relish
2 cups finely chopped celery
1 medium-size onion, finely chopped (½ cup)
1 large green pepper, finely chopped
4 teaspoons prepared mustard
2 cups mayonnaise or salad dressing
2 tablespoons prepared horseradish
¼ cup vinegar
2 envelopes unflavored gelatin
¼ cup cold water
1 cup hot water
Lettuce
Parsley
Paprika Cream, page 130

1. Combine meat, relish, celery, onion, green pepper, mustard, mayonnaise or salad dressing, horseradish, and vinegar in large bowl; toss together lightly with 2-tine fork.
2. Soften gelatin in cold water in small bowl.
3. Add hot water, stirring until gelatin dissolves; blend into ham mixture.
4. Pack firmly into 12 six-ounce custard cups or 2 two-quart molds; chill overnight in refrigerator.
5. Unmold by carefully loosening around edges of molds with knife; turn out onto serving platter; garnish with lettuce and parsley. Serve with PAPRIKA CREAM. This makes a special summer-party treat.

Meal-in-One Casserole

Bake at 375°F about 30 minutes...
Makes 4 servings

    4 ounces (half an 8-ounce package)
      elbow macaroni
    2 tablespoons butter or margarine
    2 tablespoons flour
    1 teaspoon salt
    2 teaspoons prepared horseradish
    1 teaspoon prepared mustard
    1¾ cups milk
    1¼ cups (half a 12-ounce can) diced
      corned beef
    1 cup cooked peas and carrots

1. Cook macaroni following directions on package; drain; save for Step 4.
2. Heat butter or margarine in medium-size saucepan; blend in flour, salt, horseradish, and mustard; stir in milk.
3. Cook over low heat, stirring constantly, until sauce thickens and boils 1 minute.
4. Stir sauce, corned beef, and peas and carrots into macaroni; pour into greased 2-quart baking dish.
5. Bake in moderate oven (375°F) 30 minutes, or until hot.

Dutch Bake

Bake at 425°F about 1 hour...
Makes 6 servings

    1 can (1 pound, 13 ounces) sauerkraut
    1 can (1 pound, 4 ounces) apple slices
    ½ cup brown sugar, firmly packed
    2 tablespoons vinegar
    1 small onion, finely chopped (¼ cup)
    2 tablespoons butter or margarine
    1 teaspoon caraway seeds
    1 can (1 pound) corned-beef hash
    12 whole cloves

1. Combine sauerkraut, apple slices, and their liquids with brown sugar, vinegar, and onion in baking dish, 11x7x2; dot with butter or margarine; sprinkle with caraway seeds.
2. Open can of hash at both ends; push hash out in 1 piece; cut crosswise into 6 equal slices; stud each slice with 2 whole cloves.
3. Place hash slices, clove side up, on top of sauerkraut mixture.
4. Bake in hot oven (425°F) 1 hour, or until mixture is heated through and flavors are well blended. Serve with a tossed green salad, if desired.

Piquant Corned-Beef Ring

Makes 6 servings

    1 envelope unflavored gelatin
    ½ cup cold water
    1 cup hot water
    4 beef-bouillon cubes
    3 tablespoons lemon juice
    2 teaspoons Worcestershire sauce
    1 can (12 ounces) corned beef, finely
      chopped
    1 tablespoon sugar
    1 tablespoon minced onion
    2 teaspoons prepared mustard
    2 teaspoons prepared horseradish
      Dash of cayenne

1. Soften gelatin in cold water; dissolve bouillon cubes in hot water in medium-size bowl; add softened gelatin, stirring until dissolved; add lemon juice and Worcestershire sauce; chill until syrupy.
2. Combine corned beef, sugar, onion, mustard, horseradish, and cayenne in medium-size bowl; toss together lightly with 2-tine fork.
3. Fold mixture into gelatin; turn into 1-quart ring mold lightly rubbed with salad oil; chill about 4 hours.
4. Unmold corned-beef ring onto platter; garnish with water cress, if desired.

Hot Corned-Beef Ring

Bake at 375°F about 45 minutes . . .
Makes 4 servings

    1 can (12 ounces) corned beef
    1 cup (about 2 slices) soft bread crumbs
    2 tablespoons minced onion
    2 tablespoons prepared horseradish
    1 tablespoon catsup
    1 teaspoon prepared mustard
    ½ cup milk
    2 eggs, slightly beaten

1. Break up corned beef with 2-tine fork in medium-size bowl; stir in remaining ingredients.
2. Pack into greased 1-quart ring mold or baking dish.
3. Bake in moderate oven (375°F) 45 minutes, or until set.
4. Serve with SPICED PINEAPPLE RINGS, page 139, if desired.

Harvest Hash

Bake at 375°F for 1 to 1¼ hours . . .
Makes 4 servings

    2 acorn squashes
    1 tablespoon melted butter or
        margarine
    2 teaspoons brown sugar
    Salt
    Paprika
    1 can (1 pound) corned-beef hash
    ¼ cup catsup
    1 tablespoon minced onion
    ¼ teaspoon chili powder

HARVEST HASH, *served with string beans*

1. Halve squashes lengthwise; remove seeds and strings; place halves, cut side down, in large shallow baking pan containing ¼-inch depth of water.
2. Bake in moderate oven (375°F) 45 to 60 minutes, or until tender when pierced with 2-tine fork; remove from oven; leave heat on.
3. Turn squashes right side up; brush with melted butter or margarine; sprinkle with brown sugar, salt, and paprika.
4. Break up hash with 2-tine fork in small bowl; stir in catsup, onion, and chili powder; pile into squash halves.
5. Bake 15 minutes, or until hash is heated through. Garnish with onion rings, if desired. See photograph, below.

Yankee Hash

Bake at 375°F about 40 minutes . . .
Makes 4 servings

    1 can (1 pound) corned-beef hash
    2 eggs
    1 can (about 1 pound) cream-style corn
    ¼ cup milk
    1 tablespoon chopped parsley
    1 tablespoon melted butter or
        margarine
    2 teaspoons minced onion
    1 teaspoon sugar
    ½ teaspoon salt
    ¼ teaspoon paprika
    Dash of pepper

1. Break up hash with 2-tine fork in small bowl; pack around sides of shallow 1-quart baking dish.
2. Beat eggs slightly in medium-size bowl; stir in remaining ingredients.
3. Pour mixture in center of hash-lined dish.
4. Bake in moderate oven (375°F) 40 minutes, or until center is firm.
5. Garnish with strips of pimiento and sprigs of parsley, if desired. See photograph, page 126.

125

Hash 'n' Bean Casserole

Bake at 375°F about 40 minutes ...
Makes 4 servings

1 can (1 pound) corned-beef hash
2 cans (about 1 pound each) baked red
    kidney beans or pea beans
½ cup catsup
1 medium-size onion, chopped (½ cup)
¼ cup brown sugar, firmly packed
2 tablespoons prepared mustard

1. Open can of hash at both ends; push hash out in 1 piece. Cut into 4 equal slices; halve slices.
2. Combine beans, catsup, onion, sugar, and mustard in shallow 1½-quart baking dish; top with ring of hash slices.
3. Bake in moderate oven (375°F) 40 minutes, or until bubbly hot.

Country Hash Bake

Bake at 350°F about 30 minutes ...
Makes 6 servings

2 large green peppers
1 medium-size onion
2 tablespoons fat
2 cans (1 pound each) corned-beef hash
½ cup chili sauce
¼ teaspoon thyme
6 eggs
    Paprika

1. Cut tops from green peppers; remove seeds and white membrane; slice 6 pepper rings, about ¼ inch wide.
2. Cook rings 5 minutes in ½ inch boiling salted water in small saucepan; drain; save for Step 7.
3. Chop remaining green pepper with onion; saute in hot fat in medium-size saucepan over low heat 10 to 15 minutes, or just until onion is tender.
4. Add hash, chili sauce, and thyme; toss together lightly with 2-tine fork.

Left—(top and bottom left) COUNTRY HASH
BAKE; YANKEE HASH, *page 125;*
(right) HAWAIIAN HASH PATTIES

5. Spoon mixture into baking pan, 12x8x2; level top; make 6 evenly spaced wells in hash with back of tablespoon.
6. Bake in moderate oven (350°F) 10 minutes; remove from oven; leave heat on.
7. Place green-pepper rings around wells; press down lightly.
8. Break eggs, 1 at a time, into saucer; slip 1 egg into each green-pepper ring; sprinkle eggs with paprika.
9. Return baking pan to oven; bake 20 minutes, or until eggs are cooked the way you like them. See photograph, at left.

Hawaiian Hash Patties

Bake at 350°F about 30 minutes ...
Makes 5 servings

1 can (1 pound) corned-beef hash
5 slices bacon
1 can (1 pound, 4 ounces) pineapple
    slices, drained
20 whole cloves

1. Open can of hash at both ends; push hash out in 1 piece; cut into 5 equal slices.
2. Halve bacon slices lengthwise to make 10 narrow strips.
3. PUT PATTIES TOGETHER: Cross 2 strips of bacon; place 1 pineapple slice in middle of cross; top with slice of hash and a second pineapple slice. Bring ends of bacon up and over top of stack; fasten each end to top pineapple slice with 1 whole clove.
4. Repeat with remaining bacon, pineapple, hash, and cloves to make 5 servings.
5. Place stacks about 1 inch apart in shallow baking pan.
6. Bake in moderate oven (350°F) 30 minutes, or until bacon is crisp.
7. Place stacks on heated platter; top each with spoonful of canned whole-cranberry sauce, if desired. See photograph, at left.

Sauces

Use sauces—bottled, canned, or home made—to give your meals distinction. A well-chosen sauce can make the difference between an ordinary meat and a party dish. Whatever the sauce you choose—tart, sweet, sweet-sour, spicy, or hot—make it complement the meat:

- Sweet, sweet-sour, and hot (such as mustard) sauces combine well with pork, ham, and frankfurters.
- Spicy, tart, some sweet (such as mint) and hot sauces go well with beef, veal and lamb.
- Curry sauce (a hot-type) blends well with lamb, veal, and beef.

Among the prepared sauces on your grocery-market shelves that you will want to use from the bottle or add to your home-made sauces are: soy, horseradish, hot-pepper, Worcestershire, catsup, chili sauce, thick meat sauce, barbecue, and mint sauce. Also available are many canned sauces, ready-mixed for heating. Clear consommes and condensed soups make quick sauces also.

Try your hand at making your own sauces. Subtle seasoning and long slow cooking are the secrets to success. You'll find the recipes that follow easy to make and delicious to eat.

White Sauce

Makes 1 cup sauce

	Thin	Medium	Thick
Butter or margarine	1 tablespoon	2 tablespoons	3 tablespoons
Flour	1 tablespoon	2 tablespoons	3 tablespoons
Milk	1 cup	1 cup	1 cup
Salt	½ teaspoon	½ teaspoon	½ teaspoon
Pepper	Dash	Dash	Dash

1. Melt butter or margarine in small saucepan; remove from heat.
2. Blend in flour, salt, and pepper; stir in milk slowly.
3. Cook over low heat, stirring constantly, until sauce thickens and boils 1 minute. Serve hot.

VARIATIONS

Cheddar-Cheese Sauce Add ⅓ cup grated Cheddar cheese, ½ teaspoon Worcestershire sauce, and ¼ teaspoon paprika to 1 cup WHITE SAUCE.

Horseradish Sauce Add 1 tablespoon prepared horseradish and dash of nutmeg to 1 cup WHITE SAUCE.

Stuffed-Olive Sauce Add ¼ cup chopped stuffed olives to 1 cup WHITE SAUCE.

For smooth creamy white sauce, stir milk into flour-fat mixture very slowly while pan is away from heat; cook over low heat.

Velouté Sauce

Makes 2 cups sauce

¼ cup (½ stick) butter or margarine
¼ cup sifted flour
⅛ teaspoon pepper
1 can chicken consomme
¼ cup water
1 teaspoon lemon juice

1. Melt butter or margarine in small saucepan.
2. Blend in flour and pepper; gradually stir in consomme and water.
3. Cook over low heat, stirring constantly, until sauce thickens and boils 1 minute; stir in lemon juice. Serve hot.

Spanish Sauce

Makes 2 cups sauce

¼ cup (½ stick) butter or margarine
¼ cup flour
1 can consomme
Water to make 2 cups liquid

1. Melt butter or margarine in small saucepan; brown slightly; blend in flour; cover tightly.
2. Simmer 5 minutes over *very* low heat.
3. Stir in consomme and water slowly.
4. Cook over low heat, stirring constantly, until sauce thickens and boils 1 minute. Serve hot.

Madeira-Mushroom Sauce

Makes 1½ cups sauce

1 cup **Spanish Sauce**, above
1 can (3 or 4 ounces) chopped mushrooms
¼ cup Madeira wine
½ teaspoon salt
⅛ teaspoon pepper

Combine all ingredients in small saucepan; cover; bring to boiling; reduce heat; simmer 5 minutes. Serve hot.

Florentine Sauce

Makes 1½ cups sauce

1 tablespoon butter or margarine
2 tablespoons minced onion
1 can (3 or 4 ounces) chopped mushrooms
1 cup **Spanish Sauce**, at left
2 tablespoons tomato puree
2 or 3 tablespoons dry sherry wine, if desired

1. Melt butter or margarine in small saucepan with tight-fitting cover; saute onion over low heat 5 minutes, or just until tender; add mushrooms; saute 5 minutes.
2. Stir in SPANISH SAUCE, tomato puree, and sherry wine, if desired; cover tightly.
3. Simmer 10 minutes. Serve hot.

Butter Sauces*

Plain Butter Sauce Melt ¼ cup (½ stick) sweet or salted butter in small saucepan; serve hot over broiled or fried steaks or chops.

Anchovy Butter Blend 1 teaspoon anchovy paste into ¼ cup (½ stick) melted butter.

Chives Butter Add 2 teaspoons chopped chives and 1 teaspoon lemon juice to ¼ cup (½ stick) melted butter.

Dill Butter Add 1 tablespoon chopped dill pickle to ¼ cup (½ stick) melted butter.

Garlic Butter Add ¼ teaspoon garlic salt to ¼ cup (½ stick) melted sweet butter; or ⅛ teaspoon garlic powder to ¼ cup (½ stick) melted salted butter.

Parsley Butter Add 1 tablespoon finely chopped parsley to ¼ cup (½ stick) melted butter.

Any of these sauces is delicious made with margarine.

Maitre d'Hotel Butter

Makes about ¼ cup

¼ cup (½ stick) butter or margarine
1 tablespoon lemon juice
2 teaspoons finely chopped parsley
½ teaspoon salt

Cream butter or margarine in small bowl until soft; blend in lemon juice, drop by drop, until it is absorbed; add parsley and salt; cream until fluffy. Spread on steaks and chops just before serving.

Herb Butter   Cream ¼ cup (½ stick) butter or margarine in small bowl; add ⅛ teaspoon mixed herbs (sage, marjoram, and rosemary); cream until fluffy.

Mustard Butter   Cream ¼ cup (½ stick) butter or margarine in small bowl; add 1 teaspoon prepared mustard; cream until fluffy.

Bernaise Sauce

Makes ¾ cup sauce

¼ cup (½ stick) butter or margarine
2 tablespoons hot water
2 egg yolks
1 tablespoon tarragon vinegar
1½ teaspoons finely minced onion
1 teaspoon finely minced parsley
⅛ teaspoon salt
  Dash of cayenne

1.   Melt butter or margarine in top of double boiler; stir in hot water; remove from heat.
2.   Add egg yolks; beat with rotary beater until mixture almost doubles in bulk.
3.   Stir in vinegar, onion, parsley, salt, and cayenne.
4.   Cook, stirring constantly, over hot (never boiling) water about 5 minutes, or until thick and smooth; remove from heat at once. Serve hot.

Paprika Cream

Makes about 1½ cups cream

½ cup cream for whipping
1 teaspoon paprika
½ cup mayonnaise or salad dressing

Whip cream in small bowl; fold in paprika and mayonnaise or salad dressing. Serve cold.

Curry Sauce

Makes about 2 cups sauce

2 tablespoons butter or margarine
1 medium-size onion, chopped (½ cup)
3 tablespoons flour
1½ teaspoons curry powder (vary this amount, according to taste)
½ teaspoon salt
⅛ teaspoon ground ginger
1 beef-bouillon cube, dissolved in 1 cup hot water
¾ cup milk
  Few drops bottled hot-pepper sauce
1 apple, finely diced

1.   Melt butter or margarine in medium-size frying pan; saute onion over low heat 5 minutes, or just until tender.
2.   Blend in flour, curry powder, salt, and ginger; stir in bouillon and milk slowly; add hot-pepper sauce and apple.
3.   Cook, stirring constantly, until sauce thickens and boils 1 minute; simmer until apple is tender. Use hot sauce for lamb, veal, or beef curries.

Tomato Sauce

Makes 2 cups sauce

2 cans (8 ounces each) tomato sauce
1 small onion, grated
¼ teaspoon salt
  Dash of curry powder
  Dash of ground cloves

Combine ingredients in medium-size saucepan; bring to boiling, stirring often; reduce heat; simmer 20 minutes. Serve hot.

Mushroom Sauce

Makes 2 cups sauce

    3 tablespoons butter or margarine
    ½ pound mushrooms, sliced
      Or: 1 can (3 or 4 ounces) sliced
      mushrooms, drained
    2 tablespoons flour
    ¾ teaspoon salt
    ⅛ teaspoon pepper
    1½ cups milk
      Or: Canned mushroom juice and
      enough milk to make 1½ cups
    1 or 2 tablespoons dry sherry wine, if
      desired

1.   Melt butter or margarine in small saucepan; saute mushrooms over low heat 5 to 10 minutes, or just until tender.
2.   Blend in flour, salt, and pepper; stir in milk gradually.
3.   Cook, stirring constantly, until sauce thickens and boils 1 minute; remove from heat.
4.   Add sherry wine, if desired. Serve hot.

Hot Barbecue Sauce

Makes about 2½ cups sauce

    2 cups (about 1-pound can) tomatoes
    ½ cup water
    2 tablespoons brown sugar
    2 tablespoons vinegar
    2 tablespoons Worcestershire sauce
    1 teaspoon salt
    1 teaspoon chili powder
    1 teaspoon dry mustard
    ½ teaspoon celery seeds
    1 clove of garlic, minced
      Few drops bottled hot-pepper sauce

Combine all ingredients in medium-size saucepan; bring to boiling; reduce heat; simmer 45 minutes, or until sauce thickens slightly and flavors blend. Serve hot.

Curry Barbecue Sauce

Makes about 1½ cups sauce

    1 large onion, chopped (1 cup)
    3 tablespoons lemon juice
    1 cup catsup
    ¾ cup water
    1 teaspoon curry powder
    1 teaspoon salt
    1 teaspoon brown sugar
    ¼ teaspoon ground ginger

Combine all ingredients in medium-size saucepan; cover tightly; bring to boiling; reduce heat; simmer 30 minutes, or until flavors blend. Serve hot.

Mustard Sauce

Makes about 1¼ cups sauce

    1 tablespoon butter or margarine
    2 tablespoons flour
    ½ teaspoon salt
    ¼ teaspoon paprika
    ¼ teaspoon pepper
    ¼ teaspoon Worcestershire sauce
    1 cup milk or cream
    2 tablespoons prepared mustard

1.   Melt butter or margarine in small saucepan.
2.   Blend in flour, salt, paprika, pepper, and Worcestershire sauce; stir in milk or cream slowly; add mustard.
3.   Cook over low heat, stirring constantly, until sauce thickens and boils 1 minute. Serve hot.

Hot Pineapple Sauce

Makes about 1 cup sauce

    1 can (9 ounces) crushed pineapple
    1½ tablespoons lemon juice
    2 tablespoons chopped raisins

Combine all ingredients in small saucepan; bring to boiling over low heat. Serve hot.

Apple-Raisin Sauce

Makes 1½ cups sauce

3 tablespoons brown sugar
1 tablespoon cornstarch
⅛ teaspoon salt
⅛ teaspoon cinnamon
  Dash of allspice
1 cup unsweetened apple juice
2 tablespoons lemon juice
¼ cup chopped seedless raisins
1 tablespoon butter or margarine

1. Combine brown sugar, cornstarch, salt, cinnamon, and allspice in small saucepan; stir in apple juice, lemon juice, and raisins.
2. Cook over low heat, stirring constantly, until sauce thickens and boils 1 minute.
3. Add butter or margarine; stir until melted. Serve hot with tongue, ham, or pork.

Fresh Mint Sauce

Makes ¾ cup sauce

½ cup finely chopped fresh mint
½ cup mild vinegar
¼ cup water
3 tablespoons sugar

Combine all ingredients in small bowl or jar with screw-top cover; let stand several hours to blend flavors. Serve cold with lamb or veal.

Hot Mint Sauce

Makes ½ cup sauce

½ cup mint jelly
  Grated rind of 1 lemon
2 tablespoons lemon juice
¼ teaspoon salt

Combine all ingredients in top of double boiler over hot water; beat with rotary beater until sauce is smooth and hot. Serve with lamb.

Stock

Makes 1 quart stock

2 pounds meat (beef or veal) and
  knuckle or shank bones, cracked
2 quarts water
1 medium-size onion, peeled and
  quartered
1 carrot, quartered
  Handful of celery tops
  Bouquet garni (see inside back cover)
1 teaspoon salt

1. Combine all ingredients in 4-quart kettle; cover tightly.
2. Bring to boiling; reduce heat; simmer 3 hours, or until stock is reduced to half and bones are white and porous.
3. Strain into large bowl; cool (fat will rise to top); skim.
4. Pour stock into jar; cover tightly; store in refrigerator. Use for stews, gravies, and sauces.

Crystal-Clear Stock Measure 1 quart chilled stock into medium-size saucepan; add shell and slightly beaten white of 1 egg; bring slowly to boiling, stirring constantly; boil 2 minutes; reduce heat; simmer 15 minutes, or until heavy scum forms on surface; skim; strain through double cheesecloth.

Thin Pan Gravy

1. Skim off all excess fat, leaving any meat pieces in pan.
2. Stir in ¼ to 1 cup water or stock (depending on amount of gravy you want to serve), scraping bottom of pan to loosen meat pieces and cooked-on juices.
3. Cook over low heat, stirring constantly, until gravy boils 1 minute.
4. Season to taste with salt and pepper; color with gravy flavoring, if desired.
5. Strain gravy; spoon some around meat; pass remaining in bowl.

Brown Gravy

Makes 1 cup gravy

	Thick	Thin
Fat (from cooked roast or pan-cooked meat, or added, if needed, to make gravy)	2 table-spoons	1 table-spoon
Flour	2 table-spoons	1 table-spoon
Liquid from cooked meat plus water or stock, if needed	1 cup	1 cup
Salt and pepper	to taste	to taste

1. Pour all liquid from pan into measuring cup (fat will rise to top); skim off fat; return to pan measured amount needed; save liquid for Step 4.
2. Blend in flour.
3. Place pan over low heat; stir, scraping bottom of pan to loosen meat pieces and cooked-on juices, until fat-flour mixture is rich brown.
4. Remove from heat; gradually stir in measured liquid.
5. Cook over low heat, stirring constantly, until gravy thickens and boils 1 minute.

FOR BROWN GRAVY: *Pour drippings from roasting pan into measuring cup; let fat rise; skim; return amount needed to pan.*

FOR POT ROAST GRAVY: *Stir blended flour-water mixture very slowly into hot liquid.*

6. Season to taste; color with gravy flavoring, if desired.
7. Strain gravy; spoon some around meat; pass remaining in bowl.

Pot Roast Gravy

1. Skim any excess fat from liquid in pan; strain and measure liquid; return to pan.
2. Blend 1 tablespoon flour to smooth paste with 2 tablespoons cold water in small bowl for each 1 cup liquid; gradually stir into hot liquid.
3. Cook over low heat, stirring constantly, until gravy thickens and boils 1 minute.
4. Season to taste with salt and pepper; color with flavoring, if desired.
5. Spoon some around meat; pass remaining in bowl.

Stir measured, skimmed drippings into fat-flour mixture slowly with pan removed from heat to make the blending smoother.

Meat Accompaniments

Yorkshire Pudding*

Bake at 400°F about 30 minutes . . .
Makes 6 servings

> 2 eggs
> 1 cup milk
> 1 cup sifted flour
> 1 teaspoon salt

1. Combine eggs and milk in medium-size bowl; beat with rotary beater until blended.
2. Measure flour and salt into sifter; sift into egg-milk mixture; continue beating until mixture is smooth and thick.
3. Remove ¼ cup drippings from roast-beef pan about ½ hour before roast is done; pour *hot* drippings into baking pan, 8x8x2; pour in batter.
4. Turn oven regulator to moderately hot (400°F); place pudding pan in oven.
5. Bake 30 minutes, or until lightly browned and cooked through.
6. Cut pudding into squares; place around meat on heated platter.

Fluffy Dumplings

Makes 8 large dumplings

> 2 cups sifted flour
> 4 teaspoons baking powder
> 1 teaspoon salt
> 1 cup milk

1. Measure flour, baking powder, and salt into sifter; sift into medium-size bowl.
2. Add milk all at once; stir gently just until dry ingredients are damp.
3. Drop onto top of simmering stew; cook, uncovered, 10 minutes; cover; cook 10 minutes. Serve immediately.

Some cooks prefer baking YORKSHIRE PUDDING in the same pan with the roast. Remove all pan fat but about ¼ cup. Pour batter in; turn oven regulator to moderately hot (400°F); bake 30 minutes, or until lightly browned and cooked through.

VARIATIONS

Parsley-Chives Dumplings Add ¼ cup finely chopped parsley and 1 tablespoon finely chopped chives in Step 2.

Onion Dumplings Add 3 tablespoons minced onion in Step 2.

Cheese Dumplings Add ½ cup grated cheese in Step 2.

Curried Dumplings Add 2 teaspoons curry powder in Step 1.

Potato Dumplings

Makes 8 dumplings

> 2 cups riced potatoes (about 3 medium-size)
> 1 egg, slightly beaten
> 6 tablespoons soft bread crumbs
> 6 tablespoons flour (for dumplings)
> 2 tablespoons minced onion
> 1 teaspoon salt
> ⅛ teaspoon pepper
> 2 tablespoons flour (for coating)

1. Combine potatoes, egg, bread crumbs, flour (for dumplings), onion,

CASSEROLE TOPPING QUICKIE: *Open and separate 1 package refrigerated ready-to-bake biscuit; arrange on stew in casserole; bake at 400°F 30 minutes, or until brown.*

salt, and pepper in medium-size bowl; toss together lightly with 2-tine fork.

2. Shape into 8 balls; roll in flour (for coating).

3. Drop onto top of simmering stew, or, one at a time, into large pan of boiling salted water.

4. Cook 10 to 12 minutes, or until dumplings are cooked through.

Egg Dumplings (Spaetzle)

Makes 4 servings

1½ cups sifted flour
½ teaspoon baking powder
½ teaspoon salt
⅛ teaspoon pepper
2 eggs
½ cup water
1 teaspoon finely chopped parsley

1. Measure flour, baking powder, salt, and pepper into sifter; save for Step 3.

2. Beat eggs in medium-size bowl until thick and lemon colored; add water; beat until well blended.

3. Sift and add dry ingredients; beat until batter is smooth; stir in parsley.

4. Force batter with back of mixing spoon through coarse sieve into large kettle of boiling salted water. (Dumplings look like pieces of fine noodles.)

5. Cook 6 minutes, or until dumplings are tender; drain in colander or sieve. Season with butter. EGG DUMPLINGS (Spaetzle or Spatzen) should be light and delicate.

Sour-Cream Pastry

Makes 8 rounds, each 5½ inches in diameter, or pastry for a 2-crust 8- or 9-inch pie

2 cups sifted flour
1 tablespoon sugar
1 teaspoon salt
½ cup shortening
1 egg yolk, unbeaten
1 cup sour cream

1. Measure flour, sugar, and salt into sifter; sift into medium-size bowl.

2. Cut in shortening with pastry blender or 2 knives until mixture is the texture of coarse corn meal.

3. Add egg yolk; stir in sour cream gradually; mix lightly with fork until pastry is smooth.

4. Cover bowl; chill about 2 hours, or until pastry is firm enough to handle.

5. Roll out to ⅛-inch thickness on lightly floured pastry cloth or board.

Brown-Butter Fluff Rice

Bake at 400°F for 35 to 40 minutes... Makes 4 cups

1 cup raw rice (not converted or pre-cooked)
1½ teaspoons salt
2½ cups boiling water
2 tablespoons butter or margarine

1. Spread rice in thin layer in shallow pan; bake in moderately hot oven (400°F), stirring occasionally, 15 to 20 minutes, or until golden brown.

2. Place rice in 1-quart baking dish; add salt and boiling water; cover tightly.

3. Bake in moderately hot oven (400°F) 20 minutes, or until rice is fluffy and water is absorbed.

4. Melt butter or margarine in small frying pan; heat slowly, shaking pan constantly, just until light brown and foamy. (Watch so it does not overheat and brown.)

5. Pour over rice; toss lightly.

VARIATIONS

Parmesan Fluff Rice Stir ¼ cup grated Parmesan cheese and 2 tablespoons butter or margarine into rice with salt and boiling water in Step 2; bake as above.

Curry Fluff Rice Stir ¼ teaspoon curry powder and 2 tablespoons butter or margarine into rice with salt and boiling water in Step 2; bake as above.

Potato Pancakes

Makes 8 pancakes

2 cups grated raw potatoes
1½ teaspoons salt
½ teaspoon baking powder
⅛ teaspoon pepper
⅛ teaspoon thyme
2 eggs, well beaten
1 tablespoon fat

1. Combine potatoes, salt, baking powder, pepper, and thyme in medium-size bowl; stir in eggs.
2. Spoon batter into mounds (fry half the pancakes at a time) in hot fat in large heavy frying pan; fry over low heat until brown; turn; fry until second side is brown.

Thin Pancakes

Makes 8 large thin pancakes

2 eggs
1½ cups milk
1 cup sifted flour
½ teaspoon salt

1. Beat eggs until light in medium-size bowl; add milk.
2. Measure flour and salt into sifter; sift into egg-milk mixture; beat with rotary beater until no lumps remain.
3. Ladle about ¼ cup batter at a time onto heated greaseless griddle or into lightly greased hot heavy frying pan to form large pancake.
4. Bake until brown on bottom; turn; bake until brown on other side.

Toasted Cheese Sticks

Makes 6 servings, 2 sticks each

1 roll (3 ounces) sharp process
   American cheese
6 frankfurter rolls, split

Spread cheese on cut surfaces of rolls; toast under broiler until cheese bubbles and edges of rolls are brown.

For Eye and Flavor Appeal

To give your meals that extra fillip that makes them tempting and attractive, garnish your meat dishes carefully and serve a spicy, tart, or tangy accompaniment. In choosing the garnish or accompaniment, consider the color, texture, temperature, size, and shape of your main course, then use:

- Reds, greens, and yellows; avoid purple, blue, and all artificially intensified colors. Tomato slices, pimiento, stuffed olives, parsley, water cress, and hard-cooked egg slices compliment most meats. Artificially colored fruits are often too strong in color.
- Soft-textured foods, such as STUFFED APRICOTS, page 138, with firm meats.
- Crisp foods, such as toast, with creamed or chopped meats.
- Hot accompaniments with cold meats.
- Cold accompaniments with hot meats.
- Small garnishes, such as radishes or olives, with small cuts of meat.
- Large garnishes, such as stuffed tomatoes or pepper rings, with roasts.
- A variety of shapes.

Garnish sparingly — don't overcrowd the serving platter. Allow room for carving and serving.

TO MAKE RADISH FLARES: *Remove stems and root tips from firm radishes; cut almost through crosswise into paper-thin slices; chill in ice water until the slices fan out.*

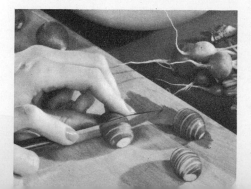

Cabbage-Pepper Relish

Makes about 3½ cups relish

- 3 cups (about ½ medium-size head) finely shredded cabbage
- 1 green or red pepper, chopped
- ½ cup vinegar
- ¼ cup water
- 1 tablespoon sugar
- 1½ teaspoons salt
- ½ teaspoon celery seeds
- ¼ teaspoon pepper
- ¼ teaspoon paprika

Combine all ingredients in large bowl; let stand 1 hour to blend flavors. Serve with hot or cold meats.

Cucumber Relish

Makes about 1 cup relish

- ¼ cup vinegar
- 2 tablespoons water
- 1 teaspoon sugar
- ½ teaspoon celery seeds
- ¼ teaspoon salt
- Dash of paprika
- Dash of pepper
- 1 cucumber, thinly sliced
- 1 medium-size onion, thinly sliced

Combine all ingredients in medium-size bowl; chill in refrigerator about 1 hour to blend flavors. Serve cold; garnish with mint or parsley, if desired.

TO MAKE CARROT CURLS: *Shave strips from scraped carrot with vegetable parer; wrap around finger to form curls; fasten on ends of wooden picks; chill in ice water 1 hour.*

Spiced Celery-Beet Relish

Makes about 1¾ cups relish

- 1 can (8 ounces) diced beets, drained
- 3 tablespoons sour cream, mayonnaise, or salad dressing
- ½ cup diced celery
- 1 teaspoon prepared horseradish
- ½ teaspoon salt
- Crisp lettuce

Combine beets, sour cream, mayonnaise, or salad dressing, celery, horseradish, and salt in small bowl; chill in refrigerator until serving time; heap in lettuce cups to serve.

Pickled Mushrooms

Makes 1¾ cups

- ½ cup brown sugar
- Grated rind of 1 orange
- ¼ cup orange juice
- 2 tablespoons lemon juice
- 1 tablespoon vinegar
- ⅛ teaspoon ground ginger
- ½ pound small mushrooms

1. Combine sugar, orange rind and juice, lemon juice, vinegar, and ginger in small saucepan; bring to boiling; add mushrooms; cover tightly.
2. Simmer 10 minutes; pour into small bowl; chill overnight.

TO MAKE FLUTED CELERY: *Cut crisp celery into 2-inch pieces; slit each end into very narrow strips, cutting almost to middle; chill in ice water until strips curl.*

Ginger Pears

Bake at 350°F for 15 to 20 minutes...
Makes 8 servings

    1 can (about 1 pound) pear halves,
      drained
    2 tablespoons chopped preserved
      ginger
      Or: ¼ teaspoon ground ginger
    ¼ cup syrup drained from preserved
      ginger
      Or: Pear syrup reduced to ¼ cup by
      boiling, mixed with ⅛ teaspoon
      cinnamon

1.   Place pear halves, hollow side up, in greased shallow baking dish.
2.   Combine chopped ginger with syrup, or ground ginger with pear syrup and cinnamon in cup; fill pear hollows with mixture.
3.   Bake in moderate oven (350°F) 15 to 20 minutes, or until pears are hot, basting once or twice during baking. Serve hot.

Cranberry-Apple Rings

Makes 4 servings, 3 rings each

    1 cup bottled cranberry-juice cocktail
    ½ cup sugar
    1 three-inch stick cinnamon
    2 tablespoons lemon juice
    3 large tart apples

1.   Blend cranberry-juice cocktail and sugar in large frying pan; add cinnamon and lemon juice; boil gently 5 minutes, or until slightly syrupy.
2.   Wash, core, and pare apples while syrup cooks; slice each into 4 thick rings.
3.   Place rings in syrup; cook over medium heat, basting often, about 10 minutes, or until apples are tender and glazed.
4.   Arrange apple rings in serving dish; pour remaining syrup over; cool.

Broiled Spiced Peaches

Makes 8 servings

Drain syrup from 1 can (1 pound, 13 ounces) peach halves. Place peaches, hollow side up, in shallow baking dish. Sprinkle lightly with cinnamon and nutmeg; place about ½ teaspoon butter or margarine in each hollow. Broil, with top of peaches 4 inches from unit or tip of flame, about 5 minutes, or until peaches are hot.

Cinnamon Pears

Bake at 350°F for 15 to 20 minutes...
Makes 8 servings

    1 can (about 1 pound) pear halves,
      drained
    ¼ cup honey
    ¼ teaspoon cinnamon

1.   Place pear halves, hollow side up, in greased shallow baking dish.
2.   Combine honey and cinnamon in cup; fill pear hollows with mixture.
3.   Bake in moderate oven (350°F) 15 to 20 minutes, or until pears are hot, basting once or twice during baking. Serve hot.

Stuffed Apricots

Makes 8 servings

    ½ cup (4 ounces) cream-style cottage
      cheese
    2 teaspoons prepared horseradish
      Salt
    1 can (about 1 pound) apricot halves,
      well drained

1.   Blend cottage cheese and horseradish in small bowl; add salt to taste.
2.   Pile seasoned cheese in centers of apricot halves. (Reserve 3 halves for decorating, if desired.)
3.   Serve as garnish with meat loaf or roast.

BROILED SPICED PEACHES

Spiced Pineapple Rings

Makes 10 slices

1 can (1 pound, 4 ounces) pineapple
  slices
1 stick cinnamon
6 whole cloves

1. Drain pineapple; save for Step 3.
2. Pour syrup into small saucepan; bring to boiling; add cinnamon and cloves.
3. Simmer pineapple slices in syrup 5 minutes, or until lightly spiced. Serve hot.

Peppermint-Pineapple Slices

Makes 4 servings

1 tablespoon melted butter or
  margarine
Few drops peppermint extract
1 can (9 ounces) pineapple slices,
  drained
1 tablespoon brown sugar

1. Combine melted butter or margarine and peppermint extract in cup; brush pineapple with mixture; let stand at room temperature 30 minutes.
2. Sprinkle pineapple with brown sugar.
3. Broil, with top of pineapple 4 inches from unit or tip of flame, 5 to 8 minutes, or until hot and slightly glazed. Serve hot.

Cranberry-Orange Relish

Makes 1 cup relish

1 cup washed fresh cranberries
½ orange, unpeeled but seeded
½ cup sugar

Put cranberries and orange through food chopper, using perforated coarse plate; combine in small bowl with sugar; chill.

Cranberry-Pineapple Relish

Makes 4 cups relish

4 cups (1 pound) washed fresh
  cranberries
1 lemon, quartered and seeded
1 can (1 pound, 4 ounces) crushed
  pineapple
¾ cup sugar

Put cranberries and lemon through food chopper, using perforated coarse plate; combine in small bowl with pineapple and sugar; chill before serving.

Aunt Elizabeth's Pineapple Pickle

Makes 4 to 6 servings

1 can (1 pound, 4 ounces) pineapple
  chunks
½ cup vinegar
½ cup sugar
1 teaspoon allspice
⅛ teaspoon salt
1 three-inch stick cinnamon
6 whole cloves

Drain pineapple; combine syrup with vinegar, sugar, allspice, salt, cinnamon, and cloves in small saucepan; bring to boiling; simmer 1 to 2 minutes; pour into small bowl; add pineapple chunks; chill overnight.

Stuffings

Bread and Butter Stuffing

Makes about 3 cups stuffing

3 cups (about 6 slices) small bread cubes
1 small onion, finely chopped (¼ cup)
2 tablespoons chopped parsley
1½ teaspoons poultry seasoning
½ teaspoon salt
⅛ teaspoon pepper
1 egg
⅓ cup melted butter or margarine

1. Combine bread, onion, parsley, poultry seasoning, salt, pepper, and egg in medium-size bowl.
2. Sprinkle butter or margarine over bread mixture; toss with fork.
3. Pack lightly into prepared pocket. This stuffing is excellent with any meat.

Brown-Rice Stuffing

Makes 2 cups stuffing

½ cup brown rice
¼ cup (½ stick) butter or margarine
1 small onion, chopped (¼ cup)
¼ pound chicken livers, chopped
½ teaspoon salt
⅛ teaspoon pepper
1 egg
2 tablespoons sherry wine

1. Cook rice in rapidly boiling salted water 20 minutes (do not overcook); drain thoroughly; place in medium-size bowl; save for Step 3.
2. Melt butter or margarine in small frying pan; saute onion over low heat 5 minutes, or just until tender; add chicken livers; saute 2 to 3 minutes.
3. Stir onions, chicken livers, salt, and pepper into rice; toss with fork.
4. Combine egg and sherry wine in small bowl; stir into rice mixture.
5. Pack lightly into prepared pocket. Use with lamb or veal.

Sweet-Potato Stuffing

Makes 4 cups stuffing

3 tablespoons melted butter or margarine
1 medium-size onion, finely chopped (½ cup)
3 cups unseasoned mashed sweet potatoes (about 3 medium-size)
1 cup (about 2 slices) small bread cubes
¼ cup chopped blanched almonds*
1 teaspoon salt
1 teaspoon poultry seasoning
⅛ teaspoon pepper
1 egg, well-beaten
¼ cup orange juice

1. Melt butter or margarine in small frying pan; saute onion over low heat 5 minutes, or just until tender.
2. Combine potatoes, bread cubes, almonds, salt, poultry seasoning, and pepper in medium-size bowl; stir in sauteed onion, egg, and orange juice.
3. Pack lightly into prepared pocket. Stuff CROWN ROAST OF PORK, page 81, with this.

Apple-Raisin Stuffing

Makes about 2 cups stuffing

1 cup (about 2 slices) coarse bread crumbs
1 cup chopped apple (1 medium-size)
¼ cup chopped raisins
½ teaspoon salt
½ teaspoon poultry seasoning
⅛ teaspoon pepper
2 tablespoons chopped onion
2 tablespoons bacon drippings or fat

1. Combine bread crumbs, apple, raisins, salt, poultry seasoning, and pepper in medium-size bowl.
2. Saute onion in hot fat in small frying pan over low heat 5 minutes, or just until tender; add to stuffing mixture; toss with fork until blended.
3. Pack lightly into prepared pocket. Stuff pork or veal with this.

*See page 141.

Pineapple-Mint Stuffing

Makes about 2½ cups stuffing

- 1 large onion, finely chopped (1 cup)
- 1 tablespoon salad oil
- 1 cup chopped celery
- 1 teaspoon crushed dried mint leaves
- 1 teaspoon salt
- ¼ teaspoon cinnamon
- 1½ cups (about 3 slices) small bread cubes
- 1 can (9 ounces) crushed pineapple, drained

1. Saute onion in hot salad oil in medium-size frying pan over low heat 10 to 15 minutes, or just until tender.
2. Add celery, mint, salt, cinnamon, bread, and pineapple; toss with fork until blended.
3. Pack lightly into prepared pocket. These flavors compliment lamb or veal.

Oyster Stuffing

Makes about 4 cups stuffing

- ¼ cup (½ stick) butter or margarine
- 1 medium-size onion, finely chopped (½ cup)
- 4 cups (about 8 slices) small bread cubes
- ½ cup chopped celery
- ½ teaspoon salt
- ¼ teaspoon pepper
- ¼ teaspoon poultry seasoning
- 1 package (12 ounces) thawed quick-frozen oysters, chopped

1. Melt butter or margarine in large heavy frying pan; saute onion over low heat 5 minutes, or just until tender; add bread cubes; saute 2 minutes, or until butter or margarine is absorbed.
2. Stir in remaining ingredients.
3. Pack lightly into prepared pocket. Try this with pork or veal.

TO CUBE BREAD FOR STUFFING: *Stack four or five slices; cut lengthwise, then crosswise with sharp knife to make amount you need.*

Apricot-Walnut Stuffing

Makes 4 cups stuffing

- ½ pound dried apricots, chopped
- 4 cups (about 8 slices) coarse dry bread crumbs
- 1 cup coarsely chopped walnuts
- 2 tablespoons chopped parsley
- 1 teaspoon salt
  Grated rind of 1 orange
- ¼ cup (½ stick) melted butter or margarine
- ½ cup hot water

1. Combine apricots, bread crumbs, walnuts, parsley, salt, and orange rind in large bowl.
2. Sprinkle butter or margarine and water over bread mixture; toss with fork until blended.
3. Pack lightly into prepared pocket. Stuff pork, veal, or lamb with this.

VARIATIONS

Prune-Walnut Stuffing Substitute ½ pound chopped, pitted, dried prunes for apricots.

To blanch and sliver almonds, pour boiling water over nuts; let stand 5 minutes, or until skins wrinkle. Drain; slip off skins. Split nuts; place, flat side down, on cutting board; cut lengthwise with sharp knife into slivers.

Index